GLOBALVIEWPOINTS

Hate Crimes

Other Books of Related Interest

At Issue Series

Minorities and the Law
White Supremacy Groups

Current Controversies Series

Islamophobia
Racism
Violence Against Women

Global Viewpoints Series [replace the book titles with these]

Civil Liberties
Discrimination
Extremism
Genocide

Opposing Viewpoints Series

Civil Liberties
Criminal Justice
Gendercide
Race in America

GLOBAL VIEWPOINTS

Hate Crimes

Barbara Krasner, Book Editor

GREENHAVEN PUBLISHING

Published in 2018 by Greenhaven Publishing, LLC
353 3rd Avenue, Suite 255, New York, NY 10010

Articles in Greenhaven Publishing anthologies are often edited for length to meet page
requirements. In addition, original titles of these works are changed to clearly present
the main thesis and to explicitly indicate the author's opinion. Every effort is made to
ensure that Greenhaven Publishing accurately reflects the original intent of the authors.
Every effort has been made to trace the owners of the copyrighted material.

Cover image: Adam Berry/Getty Images
Map: frees/Shutterstock.com

Library of Congress Cataloging-in-Publication Data

Names: Krasner, Barbara, editor.
Title: Hate crimes / edited by Barbara Krasner.
Description: New York : Greenhaven Publishing, 2018. | Series: Global viewpoints |
 Includes bibliographical references and index. | Audience: Grades 9-12.
Identifiers: LCCN ISBN 9781534501102 (library bound) | ISBN 9781534501089
 (pbk.)
Subjects: LCSH: Hate crimes--Juvenile literature.
Classification: LCC HV6773.5 H384 2018 | DDC 364.15--dc23

Manufactured in the United States of America

Website: http://greenhavenpublishing.com

Contents

Chapter 2: The Roots of Hate Crimes

Chapter 3: Hate Crimes and US Law

All Americans have a stake in stopping hate crimes, so federal legislation, state laws, and the mandated reporting of hate crimes can help everyone.

Chapter 4: Preventing Hate Crimes

Foreword

> "*The problems of all of humanity can only be solved by all of humanity.*"
> —*Swiss author Friedrich Dürrenmatt*

G lobal interdependence has become an undeniable reality. Mass media and technology have increased worldwide access to information and created a society of global citizens. Understanding and navigating this global community is a challenge, requiring a high degree of information literacy and a new level of learning sophistication.

Building on the success of its flagship series, Opposing Viewpoints, Greenhaven Publishing has created the Global Viewpoints series to examine a broad range of current, often controversial topics of worldwide importance from a variety of international perspectives. Providing students and other readers with the information they need to explore global connections and think critically about worldwide implications, each Global Viewpoints volume offers a panoramic view of a topic of widespread significance.

Drugs, famine, immigration—a broad, international treatment is essential to do justice to social, environmental, health, and political issues such as these. Junior high, high school, and early college students, as well as general readers, can all use Global Viewpoints anthologies to discern the complexities relating to each issue. Readers will be able to examine unique national perspectives while, at the same time, appreciating the interconnectedness that global priorities bring to all nations and cultures.

Material in each volume is selected from a diverse range of sources, including journals, magazines, newspapers, nonfiction books, speeches, government documents, pamphlets, organization newsletters, and position papers. Global Viewpoints is truly global, with material drawn from both international sources available in English and US sources with extensive international coverage.

Features of each volume in the Global Viewpoints series include:

- An **annotated table of contents** that provides a brief summary of each essay in the volume, including the name of the country or area covered in the essay.

- An **introduction** specific to the volume topic.

- A **world map** to help readers locate the countries or areas covered in the essays.

- For each viewpoint, an **introduction** that contains notes about the author and source of the viewpoint explains why material from the specific country is being presented, summarizes the main points of the viewpoint, and offers three **guided reading questions** to aid in understanding and comprehension.

- **For further discussion** questions that promote critical thinking by asking the reader to compare and contrast aspects of the viewpoints or draw conclusions about perspectives and arguments.

- A worldwide list of **organizations to contact** for readers seeking additional information.

- A **periodical bibliography** for each chapter and a **bibliography of books** on the volume topic to aid in further research.

- A comprehensive **subject index** to offer access to people, places, events, and subjects cited in the text, with the countries covered in the viewpoints high-lighted.

Global Viewpoints is designed for a broad spectrum of readers who want to learn more about current events, history, political science, government, international relations, economics, environmental science, world cultures, and sociology—students doing research for class assignments or debates, teachers and faculty seeking to supplement course materials, and others wanting to understand current issues better. By presenting how people in various countries perceive the root causes, current consequences, and proposed solutions to worldwide challenges, Global Viewpoints volumes offer readers opportunities to enhance their global awareness and their knowledge of cultures worldwide.

Introduction

> *"...the government of the United States, which gives to bigotry no sanction, to persecution no assistance, requires only that they who live under its protection should demean themselves as good citizens, in giving it on all occasions their effectual support."*
> —*George Washington's response to Moses Seixas, Warden of Newport Synagogue, 1790*

Incidents of hate crimes are making headlines around the world. From acts of terrorism to incendiary words on the internet, violent actions and derogatory speech demonstrate a hatred of one group or person based on some sort of bias. These biases include race, sexual orientation, gender, and ethnic origin. Targeted groups of hatred include Muslims, Jews, African-Americans, the Romani, Christians, members of the LGBT+ community, women of all races and faiths, and refugees seeking asylum. The Merriam-Webster dictionary defines hate crime as "a crime that violates the victim's civil rights and that is motivated by hostility to the victim's race, religion, creed, national origin, sexual orientation, or gender." However, how the term hate crime is interpreted varies by country and culture.

The Anti-Defamation League, a US-based non-governmental organization (NGO) which seeks to fight bias and ensure security and fair treatment of all people, created a model law that other NGOs can use to fashion their own legislation to protect targeted groups and outlaw hate crimes. Many member countries of the Organization for Security and Co-Operation in Europe, including countries in Asia, have adopted this model in some way. However, many others have yet to confront the problem.

Hate crimes have been around for millennia—as long as there have been humans to commit them. Ancient religious texts like the Bible and the Quran have been found to include many references to bias-related crime. Some groups even blame monotheism for the rise of hate crimes. In the past two centuries, the most notorious acts of race-based violence have been carried out by the Ku Klux Klan and the Nazis of Germany's Third Reich. Victims and their surviving family members had little to no recourse when it came to dealing with lynchings or the terrifying scale of the Holocaust, which exterminated more than six million Jews as well as the Romani, Russian POWs, LGBT people, and others.

The media often fanned these fires of hatred. However, in the twenty-first century, television and social media serve a dual purpose: creating a viral articulation of hatred as well as a platform for others to shut down malicious conversations. Furthermore, social media can often boost visibility of hate-based violence, such as the June 2016 mass shooting at Pulse—an Orlando, Florida, gay nightclub.

Meanwhile, the United States government continues to tackle the task of preventing and prosecuting hate crimes, setting some precedence for legislation and hate crime reporting. Though the crime rate, in general, has decreased over the last few years, the hate crime rate has increased—and legislation at the federal and state levels can be ineffective, as some viewpoints in this volume will show.

Hate crime reporting, mandated by the US Congress in 1990 through the Hate Crimes Statistics Act, is insufficient. This federal law authorizes data to be collected about crimes based on race, religion, disability, sexual orientation, and ethnicity. The Federal Bureau of Investigation (FBI) serves as the collection agent, but contributions by individual states vary and are voluntary. Yet, despite the system's shortcomings, researchers have used these statistics to analyze trends, especially race-based crime and crimes against Muslims post-9/11. The Matthew Shepard and James Byrd, Jr. Hate Crimes Prevention Act expanded the previous scope of hate crime laws to include crimes demonstrating bias against women, gays, lesbians, and transgender people. Before its passing, this law—named in honor of two victims of hate crime—was hotly debated as a bill for years in Congress. It criminalizes an act of bodily injury committed because of race, color, religion, gender/gender identity, national origin, sexual orientation, or disability and the crime affected interstate or foreign commerce. Advocates for the Hate Crimes Prevention Act (HCPA) insist the law expands protection by authorizing the US Department of Justice to investigate and prosecute hate crimes, particularly in states that don't have laws against these crimes.

Advocates against such legislation argue that the laws would be abused and that existing laws should cover so-called hate crimes. They also argue that the US Constitution guarantees equal protection and a hate crime law would violate this. On the other hand, innocent and vulnerable people belonging to certain groups have become the targets of harm, and communities become threatened even when one of its individuals undergoes an attack. As the late senator Edward M. Kennedy, of Massachusetts, stated in his support of the HCPA, "These are crimes committed against entire communities, against the nation as a whole and the very ideals on which our country was founded." Many supporters of hate crime legislation believe that crimes against those belonging to oppressed groups should face more stringent penalties.

Hate speech is another form of hate crime. There are those who staunchly believe that reigning in hate speech is a violation of the Bill of Rights' freedom of speech. Some countries have established campaigns to combat hate speech on the web. They monitor online articulations of bias against certain groups and endeavor to shut them down.

Several western countries have sought solutions for preventing and combating hate crimes. Developing comprehensive training curricula for law enforcement can help to identify cases of these crimes and outline when to take appropriate action. But prevention can also take shape at a civilian level, be it large-scale or grassroots. These preventative measures may include awareness campaigns such as "See something, say something." As the late Holocaust survivor and human rights activist Elie Wiesel said in his 1986 Nobel Peace Prize acceptance speech, "We must always take sides. Neutrality helps the oppressor, never the victim. Silence encourages the tormentor, never the tormented."

Perceptions about hate crimes vary between and within communities and countries—and laws in one country or state may not work in another. There's also one thing no amount of legislation can keep in check: fear. Fear is an obvious factor for victims of hate crimes, but it's also an underlying factor for perpetrators—including fear of change, fear of foreigners, and fear of repercussion.

The term "hate crime" has been in use since 1984, according to Merriam-Webster, but its motivations and penalties have been debated from ancient times. *Global Viewpoints: Hate Crimes* illuminates the ongoing debate, its roots and its solutions, highlighting and exploring various viewpoints from around the world.

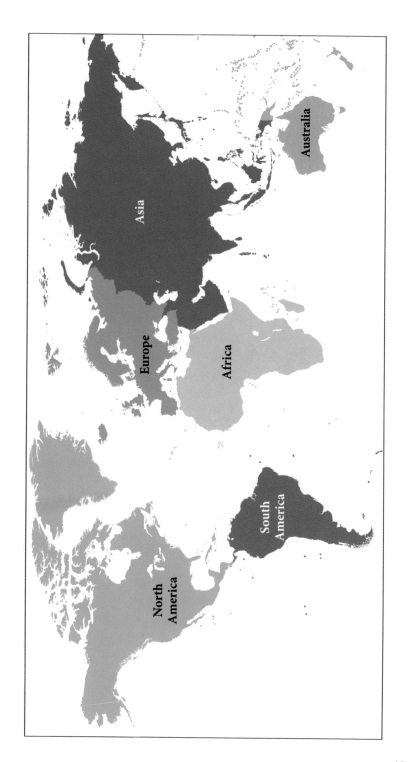

CHAPTER 1

Hate Crimes Around the World

Most Countries Still Fall Short in Fighting Hate Crimes

The Anti-Defamation League

In the following excerpted viewpoint from the Anti-Defamation League—a human rights organization that fights against prejudice and hate crimes—the Organization for Security and Co-operation in Europe (OSCE) maintains that governments have a responsibility to respond to hate-based violence. That responsibility includes collecting data, gaining cooperation from communities and human rights groups, as well as availing themselves of the training resources OSCE has to offer. However, only 36 of 57 participating members are living up to their responsibility in some way.

As you read, consider the following questions:

1. Is it important for participating states to follow OSCE guidelines?
2. What is the value of collecting hate crime data?
3. Should this data always be publicly shared?

Overview

Violent hate crime continues to plague the Organization for Security and Co-operation in Europe (OSCE) region. In the summer of 2014, anti-Israel sentiment was used as a pretext for an alarming wave of anti-Semitic hatred and violence in France, Germany, Italy and elsewhere in Europe. Russia's law banning so-

"Hate Crime Response in the OSCE Region," The Anti-Defamation League (www.adl.org), December 2, 2014. Reprinted by permission.

called "gay propaganda" continues to create a hostile environment for lesbian, gay, bisexual, and transgender (LGBT) people in that country; several of Russia's neighbors are considering similar laws. In many other parts of Europe, too, LGBT persons are targeted by violence that often goes unreported or altogether ignored by police. Muslims and their institutions continue to be targeted for violence and people of African and Middle Eastern origin have been the victims of serious racist and xenophobic violence. In many parts of the region, Roma remain the most marginalized and face routine violence and harassment with little recourse to justice.

Openly anti-Semitic, anti-Muslim, racist or homophobic far-right political parties have gained strength in local and national elections and, in 14 countries, such parties won seats in the European Parliament in May 2014. Racist violence associated with these parties has not stopped their rise in the polls. Most stunning is the case of the neo-Nazi Golden Dawn party, which polled third in the May European Parliament elections in Greece despite its entire leadership being under indictment for organizing a three-year wave of dozens of violent attacks—including murders—targeting dark-skinned undocumented migrants. All of these trends threaten to undermine the values on which the OSCE is built.

Governments have a responsibility to respond to hate crime violence. They can enhance their effectiveness through close cooperation with community and human rights groups, as well as by availing themselves of the training and other resources of the OSCE Office for Democratic Institutions and Human Rights (ODIHR). At the political level, the 57 participating States of the OSCE have adopted Ministerial and other decisions—most recently in 2009—that have established commitments to combat hate crimes, including by improving their efforts to collect data and adopt adequate hate crime legislation. A high-level commemorative event on anti-Semitism held in November 2014 in Berlin highlighted an alarming rise in hatred and violence and produced concrete recommendations for action steps from both governments and civil society participants, which should be brought forward formally into the work of the OSCE in 2015. The ODIHR assists participating States in the implementation of these commitments through the range of reporting, know-how, tools, and training resources.

The findings of the ODIHR's 2013 annual report on hate crime reporting across the region reveal that, some progress notwithstanding, participating States continue to fall short in their commitments to combat hate crime.

The annual report is an important tool in understanding the nature and frequency of hate crime across the OSCE region. However, such reporting is undermined when states either do not collect such data at the national level or fail to contribute their findings to the ODIHR on a timely basis.

For this latest report, only 36 (of 57 participating States) submitted completed information to ODIHR for 2013. While this is an increase from prior years, 72 percent of the participating States either did not report at all or reported zero crimes for their country. In addition, the report includes information from 109 nongovernmental organizations (NGOs) covers incidents for 45 countries.

Since 2008, more than 50 of the 57 participating States have at some point indicated that they do collect some hate crime data, although far fewer have responded consistently to ODIHR's annual requests for timely and updated information. The quality of the data collected and submitted is in most cases insufficient and falls short of what States have committed to collect. Table 2 in this document, where black dots represent the absence of information, is the best visual of the failure of many States to meet basic data collection commitments.

Even where data is submitted, it is in many cases of questionable value to policy making. Even countries that have made efforts to establish more robust monitoring systems generally do not disaggregate the data to indicate the type of crime or group targeted—limiting its usefulness to serve as a tool to develop sound policies to protect those vulnerable to bias- motivated attacks. Few countries provide information on the criminal justice response to these crimes.

Over the last several years, States have made important progress in their commitments to adopt hate crime laws, although six States still have not done so. The adoption of the law, though, is only the first step—implementation remains weak and most States that have such laws often fall short of extending protection to frequently targeted groups.

NGO Contributions

Importantly, ODIHR's report makes use of information from NGOs and inter-governmental organizations (IGOs) to fill broad data gaps left by the absence of official reporting. ODIHR should be credited with the level of outreach it has conducted with such groups with a view to bolstering the level of reporting on hate crimes from a variety of sources.

For this report, NGOs contributed as follows:

- 37 NGOs covering 25 States on racist and xenophobic hate crime.
- 16 NGOs covering 11 States on hate crime against Roma and Sinti.
- 35 NGOs covering 28 States on anti-Semitic hate crime.
- 25 NGOs covering 21 States on anti-Muslim hate crime.
- 11 NGOs covering 27 States on hate crime against Christians and followers of other religions.
- 50 NGOs covering 35 States on hate crime against LGBT persons.
- 12 NGOs covering six States on hate crime against people with disabilities and other groups.

Group I States: No Public Hate Crime Data Collected

No Hate Crime Data Available

The Former Yugoslav Republic of Macedonia indicated that they do not compile any data on hate crime incidents, while Holy See, Malta, Mongolia, San Marino, and Turkmenistan did not indicate whether or not they collect hate crime data. Holy See submitted information in 2013 on hate crimes against Christians in other OSCE participating States.

No Public Data Available

At least 10 States—Croatia, Estonia, Ireland, Italy, Kyrgyzstan, Latvia, Lithuania, Luxembourg, Montenegro, and Turkey—claim to collect data, but either do not publicize it or make it available to the public only upon request. Such a policy essentially eliminates the public from discussions about the nature and scale of hate crimes, as well as measures taken by the government to combat them. In addition to informing policymakers, data on violent hate crimes should be made publicly available so as to better involve civil society in a robust public debate on effective responses.

Recommendations

- For those countries in which no hate crime data is available, undertake to establish a system for the collection of hate crime data.

- Make hate crime data, including the data submitted to the ODIHR and other international institutions, available to the public.

Group II States: No or Limited Data Submitted to ODIHR for 2013

Nothing Submitted to ODIHR

25 States—Albania, Armenia, Azerbaijan, Canada, Cyprus, Denmark, Estonia, Georgia, Holy See, Iceland, Kazakhstan, Luxembourg, Former Yugoslav Republic of Macedonia,

Malta, Monaco, Mongolia, Montenegro, Netherlands, Portugal, Russia, San Marino, Slovenia, Tajikistan, Turkmenistan, and Ukraine—did not submit data and/or official statistics on hate crimes to the ODIHR for 2013.

Recommendations

- Conduct an inquiry into the potential shortcomings in existing reporting and data collection systems.

- Make complete hate crime data available to ODIHR and other international institutions.

- Train police to identify and properly record bias-motivated incidents and to forge links with community groups.

- Reach out to NGOs and develop programs to enhance reporting of hate crimes.

Group III States: Data Is Insufficiently Disaggregated According to Bias

One of the goals of effective systems of data collection is to identify the groups that are most affected by hate crimes—a process that hopefully guides the creation of effective policies aimed at protecting any such vulnerable groups. However, few States disaggregate hate crime data on the basis of the bias motivations or victims' characteristics. Even fewer actually submit data to back up those claims.

Recommendations

- Develop monitoring systems that provide disaggregated data on the characteristics of the victims or on the bias motivations.

- Make disaggregated hate crime data available to the ODIHR and to the public.

Group IV States: Data Is Insufficiently Disaggregated Between Violent Crimes, Incitement, Discrimination, and other Violations

Many States claim to disaggregate data by the type of crime to distinguish between violent crime, verbal threats and insults, and incitement to hatred. However, such data is rarely available publicly. Only 12 States disaggregated this data in a manner we deem satisfactory for monitoring and evaluation purposes. In most cases, either this data was not submitted to the ODIHR at all or States did not disaggregate sufficiently by incident (e.g. hate speech and hate crimes are not disaggregated).

Due to insufficient disaggregation of incidents between violent crimes, incitement, discrimination, and other violations, it is difficult to accurately assess the nature of the problem in a given country and to identify the targeted measures that would be most effective.

Recommendations

- Classify data on the basis of all types of bias motivated crime, disaggregating between violent crimes and nonviolent criminal violations.

- Make hate crime data—disaggregated by crime type— available to the ODIHR and to the public.

Group V States: Lack of Data on Prosecution and Sentencing

Statistics for sentencing and prosecutions are necessary to assess the government response to hate crimes.

However, the vast majority of participating States did not submit data regarding prosecutions in hate crime cases in 2013.2 Thus, though there are an increasing number of States that are adopting hate crime laws, there is little evidence to evaluate how those laws are used.

Recommendation:

- Establish and/or enhance existing monitoring systems to disclose the record of both prosecutions of hate crime cases and the use of sentence enhancement provisions.

Group VI States: Existence of Hate Crime Laws in Criminal Codes

A growing number of the 57 countries in the OSCE region are adopting criminal laws to expressly address violent hate crimes, largely in the form of penalty enhancement provisions, since the ODIHR began to track the issue. At present, there are more than

50 countries in which legislation treats at least some bias-motivated violent crime as a separate crime or in which one or more forms of bias is regarded as an aggravating circumstance that can result in enhanced penalties.

However, 21 OSCE participating States still have no express provisions defining bias as an aggravating circumstance in the commission of a range of violent crimes against persons. They are: Belgium, Bulgaria, Estonia, Germany, Holy See, Hungary, Iceland, Ireland, Kyrgyzstan, Luxembourg, Malta, Monaco, Mongolia, Netherlands, Norway, Poland, Portugal, Slovakia, Slovenia, Switzerland, and Turkey.

Data from government bodies, NGOs and media in several of these countries indicate that violent hate crimes are occurring, but criminal justice authorities are unable to address the bias nature of the crime because they lack a legislative basis to do so.

All laws in countries where legislation addresses bias-motivated violence as a separate crime or as an aggravating circumstance cover bias based on race, ethnicity, and/or national origin, and most also cover religious bias. Hate crime legislation extending to bias motivated by animus based on sexual orientation, though increasing, exists in only 29 States—Andorra, Austria, Belgium, Canada, Croatia, Cyprus, Denmark, Estonia, Finland, France, Georgia, Greece, Hungary, Iceland, Lithuania, Luxembourg, Malta, Netherlands, Norway, Portugal, Romania, San Marino, Serbia, Slovakia, Slovenia, Spain, Sweden, United Kingdom, and the United States—disability in only 18—Andorra, Austria, Belgium, Canada, Finland, Georgia, Greece, Hungary, Lithuania, Luxembourg, Former Yugoslavian Republic of Macedonia, Netherlands, Norway, Romania, Spain, Slovenia, United Kingdom, and the United States—and gender identity in 10—Croatia, France, Georgia, Greece, Hungary, Malta, Portugal, Serbia, United Kingdom, and the United States.

Recommendations

- Enact laws that establish specific offenses or provide enhanced penalties for violent crimes committed because of the victim's race, religion, ethnicity, sexual orientation, gender, gender identity, mental and physical disabilities, or other similar status.

- Concrete steps to begin this process could involve utilizing the ODIHR publication *Hate Crime Laws: a Practical Guide* as a basis for a training or consultation among experts and officials across relevant ministries.

[…]

Recent 2014 Examples of Hate Crimes and Incidents

- In September, Ekaterina Khomenko, a lesbian dance instructor in St. Petersburg, **Russia**, was found murdered. Ekaterina's body was found in the driver's seat of her car with the engine running and headlights on; her throat had been slashed. In the days leading up to her murder a known extremist had posted threats and hate speech to her profile page on Russia's leading social media platform, Vkontakte. com.

- On August 2, in Athens, **Greece**, a Pakistani man was attacked and brutally beaten. He was taking a bus home from work when another passenger asked his nationality and if he had ever been attacked by Golden Dawn. The alleged assailant then made a phone call and, once both had stepped off the bus, appeared to summon four men in black shirts who attacked and beat the Pakistani man, breaking his jaw. An Iranian man was attacked only five days later, also in Athens; two assailants asked him where he was from and, when he answered, stabbed him twelve times. He also required hospitalization. Despite the fact that many Golden Dawn leaders are on trial for a series of racist killings and other attacks over the past several years, Golden Dawn gained nearly 10 percent of the vote in national elections in May, the third highest of any Greek political party.

- Violence against Jews and Jewish institutions around the world occurred during Israel's operation in Gaza this summer. In **France** on July 13, during a large anti-Israel demonstration, two synagogues were attacked. Dozens of demonstrators broke off and tried to attack the Synagogue de la Roquette in Paris, while other demonstrators tried to enter the synagogue at Rue des Tournelles. Anti-Semitic slogans were reported in both incidents and chants of "Death to the Jews!" were heard during the demonstration. A week later in Sarcelles,

France, a kosher store was attacked with Molotov cocktails during an illegal anti-Israel demonstration and several other stores were damaged in the violence. In **Germany**, on July 12, anti-Semitic chants of "Jews to the gas" were shouted during an anti-Israel demonstration in Gelsenkirchen on July 12, 2014. On the same day in the **United Kingdom**, following a pro-Palestinian rally, occupants in a group of cars driving through the Jewish neighborhood of Broughton Park in Manchester shouted and swore at Jewish pedestrians with slogans that included "Heil Hitler". Cans and eggs were thrown at Jewish pedestrians from at least two of the cars.

- On June 13, approximately fifty people attacked a Roma teenager and pulled him away from his family in **France**. The gang, whose members carried guns, machetes, and spears, took the teenager to a basement where they beat him, burned him, and poured battery acid into his mouth, dissolving part of his jaw. They left him for dead in a shopping cart. Police suspect that the attack was in retaliation for a series of burglaries nearby. The teenager was in a coma for over a month. No charges have been filed.

- In June, a Jewish cemetery in Tatabanya, **Hungary**, was vandalized and slogans including "Stinking Jews" and "There was no Holocaust but there will be" were painted on gravestones. The openly anti-Semitic and racist political party Jobbik gained more than 20 percent of the vote in the 2014 Hungarian parliamentary elections.

- In June, in Belfast, **Northern Ireland**, two Pakistani men were attacked in their home by anti-Islamic rioters. The mob smashed their windows and returned a few hours later to enter the home and physically assault them. One man was hospitalized. The attacks came in the weeks after an evangelical pastor called Islam "spawn of the devil." Northern Ireland's first minister Peter Robinson defended these remarks, saying that he also did not trust Muslims.

Mr. Robinson later said he did not intend to cause offense. Two individuals were arrested in connection to the attacks.

- An unnamed foreign tourist was found murdered in the resort city of Yevpatoria in Crimea, **Ukraine**, in late June. Authorities claimed that the body, which was left prominently in front of a monument to World War II Marines, showed signs of a violent death. Police are seeking multiple suspects who they believe were motivated by homophobia. According to one official, "Most likely, the cause of the murder is related to his unconventional hobbies."

- On May 24, Mehdi Nemmouche, a French radical Islamist, opened fire inside the Jewish Museum in Brussels, **Belgium**, killing four people. He was arrested six days later, carrying weapons and materials related to the Islamic State terror group.

- In March, a prominent member of the "Football Fans Against Homophobia" campaign in **Sweden** was left in a coma after he and five others were attacked by assailants carrying knives. The attackers were members of the Svenskarnas Parti, or Party of Swedes, a National Socialist party that States that only people of "western and genetic cultural heritage" should be Swedish citizens. This incident was one in a growing number of racist, homophobic, and xenophobic attacks in Sweden. Cars owned by individuals with names that sound foreign have been vandalized with pictures of swastikas, and on February 3 a woman in Finspång returned home to find an ax in her door next to a drawing of a Star of David and the word "Disappear."

- On January 17, a 28 year-old Yeshiva student was beaten and stabbed by three youths as he was walking home from synagogue services in Kiev, **Ukraine**. He managed to return to the synagogue where he collapsed. He was taken to the hospital and underwent emergency surgery.

On the Stoning of LGBT Citizens in Bulgaria

Two years ago, I was asked to speak at the opening of the first Baltic Pride Parade in Vilnius, Lithuania. It was a chilling experience. When I arrived in that European Union member state, the organisers greeted me with disappointment. A court had issued an order banning the parade, which was to be a proud celebration of the lesbian, gay, bisexual, and transgender community. Members of parliament had also written an open letter claiming that a Pride Parade would be harmful to children and an affront to Lithuania's moral standards.

The march was allowed to go ahead the next day. However, as I joined the peaceful demonstrators, singing songs and waving rainbow flags—I was astonished to witness hundreds of aggressive opponents screaming and shouting, throwing Molotov cocktails and stones at us. Among them were three members of parliament. One of them broke through the police cordon and physically attacked the organiser of the parade.

Unfortunately, pride parades have not yet become dull, it seems. Take, for instance, the LGBT Pride Parade planned for June 30 in Sofia, Bulgaria. On June 6, Father Evgeni Yanakiev of the Bulgarian Orthodox Church was quoted in the newspaper Standart as saying: "Our whole society must, in every possible way, oppose the gay parade that is being planned."

The call to stone gay people is not only incitement to commit a crime and disrupt public order, but also a heinous threat to the security of peaceful EU citizens who want nothing more than to enjoy their freedom of assembly and expression.

—*"Bulgaria: 'Chilling'"Calls for Stoning of LGBT Citizens in Bulgaria," by Boris Dittrich, Human Rights Watch, June 28, 2012.*

In the United Kingdom, the Government Takes Measures Against Hate Crimes

Home Office, United Kingdom

In the following excerpted viewpoint, the government of the United Kingdom introduces its initiative to challenge report, and stop hate crimes. It argues that each individual has the right to live without fear of abuse or attack. The authors detail the importance of preventing hate crime by challenging biased attitudes, encouraging more reporting and improved access to support resources, improving response to hate crime through training, and handling offenders in an effective manner. The Home Office is the United Kingdom's major department handling crime, drugs, immigration, and other homeland matters.

As you read, consider the following questions:

1. Which aspects of hate crime should take priority— challenging it, reporting it, or stopping it? Why?
2. What value does the viewpoint have coming from the Minister of State for Crime Prevention?
3. What is the benefit of reporting on the progress of the initiative?

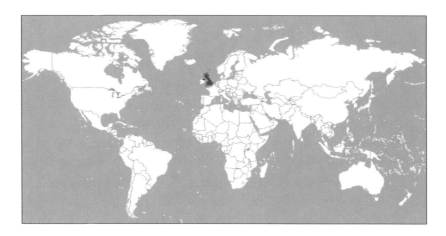

Challenge It, Report It, Stop It: Delivering the Government's hate crime action plan

Ministerial Foreword

Living without the fear of being abused or attacked because of who you are is a basic human right and one we all share. However, in 2012/13, 42,236 hate crimes were recorded by police forces in England and Wales. That is both depressing and unacceptable and shows that far too many people's lives are devastated by hostility and hatred.

I believe that we all have a responsibility to challenge the attitudes and behaviours that foster hatred. Intervening early to raise awareness and to promote positive narratives, for example, with children and young people, within professional sports, through social media networks and many other channels can make a real difference.

The Coalition Government has made good progress in delivering its commitments to tackle hate crime since 'Challenge it, Report it, Stop it' was published in March 2012, and we continue to drive forward work focused on our three core principles: to prevent hate crime happening in the first place; to increase reporting and access to support; and to improve the operational response to hate crime.

We now have a better understanding of hate crime, and have provided direct support to frontline professionals to help build victims' confidence to come forward. The police have also improved the way they record hate crimes, and we continue to publish Official Statistics, which tell us more about the types of hate crimes that are committed and where those crimes are happening.

However, the Crime Survey highlights that victims are still reluctant to report incidents to the police. It is vital that we continue to work closely with our partners and voluntary sector organisations to ensure that victims feel confident in coming forward, particularly those victims who can feel isolated, including disabled and transgender people, Roma, Gypsy and Traveller communities and new migrants. I am determined to do more to tackle the root cause of under-reporting of hate crimes.

Our strengthened legislative framework will ensure that the suite of aggravating factors available to the courts at the sentencing stage is consistent across the five monitored strands of hate crime. We will also shortly consider the findings from the Law Commission's consultation on the case for extending the existing stirring up hatred and aggravated offences.

Addressing anti-Muslim hatred remains a central theme and our dialogue with local communities is already underway through the roll out of a number of regional roadshows. These events provide the opportunity to promote our work and to allow us to explore what more we can do to tackle the issue.

Understanding different forms of disability hate crime, particularly against people with learning disabilities and those with an autism spectrum disorder, has been at the forefront of our efforts due to the excellent work of the Equality and Human Rights Commission and key disabled people's organisations. Ensuring that the response to disability hate crime is tailored to victims' needs will be important when local agencies are dealing with cases.

We have been clear that local areas must take the lead in tackling hate crime. We know that some local areas are making a real impact on the ground and we are keen to share such examples of innovative approaches more widely.

We are making real progress in tackling hate crime, but there is still much to do to confront the hatred and hostility that still exists in our society.

Norman Baker MP
Minister of State for Crime Prevention

Executive Summary

This Government believes that everyone should be free to live their lives without fear of abuse or attack because of who they are. All crime is wrong, but crime that is motivated by hostility or hatred towards the victim is particularly corrosive. It can have devastating consequences for victims and their families, but can also divide communities. In March 2012, we published 'Challenge it, Report it, Stop it', the Government's plan to tackle hate crime. The plan brought together action by a range of departments and agencies under three core principles:

- To prevent hate crime—by challenging the attitudes that underpin it, and intervening early to prevent it escalating;

- To increase reporting and access to support—by building victim confidence and supporting local partnerships; and

- To improve the operational response to hate crimes—by better identifying and managing cases, and dealing effectively with offenders.

We committed to reviewing the plan, to assess progress in delivering those actions and to ensure it addressed new and emerging issues. This report provides an overview of our achievements since the plan was published, and case study examples demonstrating how work is being delivered locally. It also highlights areas that are evolving as we drive our agenda forward, and what we will do to tackle those issues.

Progress So Far

Two years on, we have delivered many of the actions under our three core principles, and we are making good progress on the others.

We are building the evidence base on hate crime, including delivering on our coalition commitment to improve police recording of hate crimes under the five monitored strands—disability, race, religion/belief, sexual orientation and transgender-identity. The latest figures show that in 2012/13 42,236 hate crimes were recorded by police forces in England and Wales, which is broadly similar to the level of recording for 2011/12. We are challenging the attitudes and behaviours that drive hate crime, and have strengthened a legal framework which is already regarded as one of the most robust in the world in protecting people from hatred and bigotry.

We have also invested over £2.2 million providing direct support to professionals at the frontline, to voluntary sector organisations and to victims of hate crime.

However, there is more we need to do to stop hate crime happening, and to protect and support victims and their families, and communities. In contrast to police figures, the findings from the combined Crime Survey for England and Wales in 2011/12 and 2012/13 on the extent of hate crime, estimate that on average there are around 278,000 hate crimes each year highlighting the importance of working to tackle under-reporting. That is why we continue to work closely with a wide range of voluntary sector, community representatives, frontline organisations, and with the Government's Independent Advisory Group on Hate Crime, who provide valuable insight into the day-to-day experience of hate crime.

A New Approach

'Challenge it, Report it, Stop it' placed hate crime within the Government's wider approach to cutting crime, based on freeing professionals from top-down targets and making the police democratically accountable to the communities they serve, including through the election of Police and Crime Commissioners (PCCs). The action plan was clear that local strategies for tackling hate crime should reflect the needs and priorities of local victims and communities, rather than priorities imposed by Whitehall. The role of Government was to set a national direction and support those locally-led efforts.

Police and Crime Commissioners have now been in place for over a year, and are focussing their police forces on the issues that matter most to local people. We know that hate crime is featured as a priority in many PCCs' Policing and Crime Plans, and PCCs are challenging other local partners to work better together to support victims. From October 2014, PCCs will also be responsible for commissioning the majority of support services for victims of crime, based on local needs and priorities.

In December 2013, we brought into force a new Code of Practice for Victims of Crime setting out the information and services that victims of crime will receive from criminal justice agencies in England and Wales. The Code includes an enhanced level of service for victims of the most serious crime, including victims of hate crime and persistently targeted, vulnerable or intimidated victims.

Emerging Challenges

Since the publication of the action plan a number of issues have emerged or have continued to evolve. We are working across Government, with our partners, the voluntary sector and internationally to take action in the following areas:

Disability hate crime—the Equality and Human Rights Commissions Inquiry into disability-related harassment, and the horrendous abuse that took place at Winterbourne View Hospital, provide some salutary lessons on the way the 'system' can fail victims of disability hate crime. The Government responded to the Commission's interim report, and more recently published a progress update setting out the steps we and our partners are taking to tackle disability hate crime. The report on Winterbourne View

Hospital set out national action to transform care and support for people with learning disabilities, including measures to ensure staff are aware of disability hate crime, and know how to raise concerns.

Hate crime online—the task of removing hate material from mass media channels such as the internet, whilst also protecting freedom of expression, is a challenging one. Over the last few years we have seen huge changes in the use of social media as a means of communication. Whilst in this context, we have seen it used as a means to spread harmful and negative messages, we recognise that it can also be used in a positive way to counter those negative narratives.

Experience tell us that many Internet Service Providers (ISPs), including all reputable UK ISPs, will remove on request material that is illegal or where it breaches their wider terms and conditions for acceptable use. However, we also have many examples of providers and hosts, including those based overseas, who have declined to remove material which would be illegal in the UK.

We are working with the police and the Independent Advisory Group on Hate Crime to build relationships with leading social media providers and to improve their response to offensive and illegal hate-related content online. This has involved supporting the international Working Group of the Inter-Parliamentary Coalition to Combat Antisemitism. The Group has brought leading social media companies together with politicians, civil society, academics and subject experts to find collaborative solutions to reduce the harm caused by hate on the internet in a way that puts the companies at the heart of the solutions and seeks to work within the diverse global legislative frameworks.

We are also working more closely internally to ensure we are linking with policy and operational areas where there are cross-cutting issues relating to online crime, for example, making links with online extremism.

The Director for Public Prosecutions has also published guidelines for prosecuting cases involving social media communications, including hate crimes. These guidelines provide

A Response to the Government's
Hate Crime Action Plan

At the time of writing, we have just witnessed yet more atrocities across France and Germany and, yet again, words fail us as to why these senseless, cowardly acts keep on happening and our thoughts and condolences go out to all the people involved and affected.

On the same day, the British Government reaffirmed its pledge to tackling Hate Crime in the UK, with newly appointed Home Secretary, Amber Rudd, announcing the **Government's Action Plan on Hate Crime.**

Stop Hate UK welcomes this plan and is pleased to see the Government moving to recognise the seriousness of such crimes and why there has to be a zero tolerance approach to any form of Hate Crime.

No one should want to live in a society filled with hate and it should not be commonplace, in today's world, to simply accept these horrendous acts as 'part of life'. Hate crime, in any form, is not welcome here and we must stand together to tackle it and rid our society of such harrowing incidents.

Racism, hate, intolerance—call it what you will—is still an odious undercurrent in the UK and, for some, the referendum result was merely a vehicle to jump on the back of and vent draconian views, like they suddenly had a right to do, which, of course, they did not.

It is the Government's duty to spearhead the campaign against hate, working with organisations, like Stop Hate UK, to set out a clear message of zero tolerance, so we are pleased to see the Action Plan's pledge of help where it is needed, particularly the promise of new training and advice for schools and journalists, improving victims' support and creating a database of racist symbols so police can recognise them.

"Response to Government Hate Crime Action Plan," Stop Hate UK, July 28, 2016.

clarity to prosecutors and the police on the criminal thresholds for prosecutions.

We have commissioned the Society of Editors to look into the moderation of user generated content with the aim of publishing a good practice guide in the Spring 2014. Early indications suggest that the majority of publications that have an online presence, 'do' moderate, and that most news website publishers take moderation seriously and invest considerable resources in it. They are aware of the reputational and possible legal implications of unsuitable material being posted on their sites, coupled with the determination of certain users to post abusive comments.

Extremism and hate crime—extremism can flourish where different parts of a community remain isolated from each other. More integrated communities will be more resilient to the influence of extremists.

Extremism is less likely to be tolerated by communities which come together to challenge it. Britain is stronger because of its open, multi-faith and multi-racial communities. It is important that this effort is led locally by communities who know their areas best.

However, the Government also has an important role to play in tackling all forms of extremism. Last December, the Prime Minister published Tackling Extremism in the UK, the report from the Extremism Task Force (ETF). The ETF was established in the wake of the horrific murder of Drummer Lee Rigby in Woolwich, to identify gaps in our approach and to agree practical steps to address all forms of extremism. The report sets out what the Government and its partners will do to contribute to that effort. In addition to those commitments we will continue work to confront the extremist narrative.

Next Steps

We believe that the three core principles of: preventing hate crime; increasing reporting and access to support; and improving the operational response to hate crimes are still the right ones. We will continue to work towards these objectives over the remainder of this Parliament and will review 'Challenge it, Report it, Stop it' again to assess progress at the end of the plan's cycle.

In South Africa, Xenophobic Violence Results from Competition for Resources

South African History Online

In the following viewpoint from South Africa History Online, the authors argue that race-based attacks in South Africa impact foreign nationals seeking economic and political asylum, a trend that began in the 1980s, and everyone else living in South Africa. The authors claim fear of foreigners and competition for resources motivate these attacks. Complicating the situation is that the number of migrants cannot be easily quantified. South Africa History Online is an educational outreach project dedicated to the country's history and its establishment of freedom and democracy.

As you read, consider the following questions:

1. How many refugees from Mozambique found asylum in South Africa in the 1980s?
2. Of the hate crimes presented here, who were, by and large, the perpetrators?
3. What announcement did the Zulu king make in March 2015?

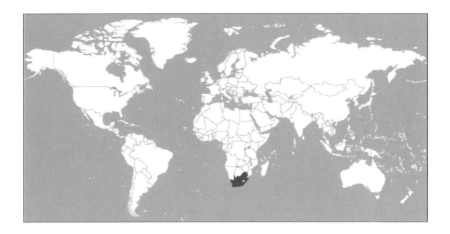

Xenophobic violence in democratic South Africa

Xenophobic violence against foreign nationals in South Africa has worsened. South Africa witnessed widespread xenophobic attacks since 1994 in provinces such as Gauteng, Western Cape, Free State, Limpopo and KwaZulu Natal. There has been this and much speculation of the c auses and triggers of the violence. A number of reports have highlighted various issues contributing to xenophobia; some of which include poor service delivery and competition for resources. The type of leadership within communities might have an impact on whether or not xenophobic attacks occur in certain communities, which talks to issues of governance. The issue is not only about foreign nationals and their rights, but about the safety of all who live in South Africa. Most incidents of violent attacks have been carried out by black South Africans.

Overview

The history of refugees and asylum seekers in South Africa dates back to the 1980s when the country was home to a number of Mozambican refugees, an estimated 350,000, of whom approximately 20% have since returned home. South Africa did not recognise refugees until 1993 and when it became a signatory to the United Nations (UN) and Organisation of African Unity Conventions on Refugees in 1994. The number of refugees and asylum seekers in South Africa has increased in the past years, puts the total number of cross-border migrants in this category at not more than 150 000. The issue regarding the number of undocumented migrants in the country has proved to be a controversial one in South Africa. Central to this debate is the unquantifiable nature of this group of migrants together with a number of credible myths widely accepted as reality in South African society.

South Africa is Africa's most industrialised country, and it attracts thousands of foreign nationals every year, seeking refuge from poverty, economic crises, war and government persecution in their home countries. While the majority of them are from elsewhere on the continent, such as Zimbabwe, Malawi, Democratic Republic of Congo, Somalia and Ethiopia, many also come from Pakistan and Bangladesh. Xenophobia is generally defined as 'the deep dislike of non-nationals by nationals of a recipient state.' This definition is also used by the South African Human Rights Commission (SAHRC). Xenophobia is also a manifestation of racism. Racism and xenophobia support each other and they share prejudiced discourses. They both operate on the same basis of profiling people and making negative assumptions. The profiling in the case of racism is on the basis of race, in the case of xenophobia on the basis of nationality.

When the xenophobic violence in South Africa occurred, the victims were not only foreigners in the sense of a different nationality are attacked but in fact everybody not belonging to the dominant ethnic groups in the main cities, Zulu or Xhosa, was attacked. Members of smaller ethnic groups in South Africa are also viewed as foreigners by fellow South Africans. White people are not viewed as foreigners in the context of xenophobic violence. There had been attacks on South Africans who 'looked foreign' because they were 'too dark' to be South African.

Reasons for the attacks differ, with some blaming the contestation for scarce resources, others attribute it to the country's violent past, inadequate service delivery and the influence of micro politics in townships, involvement and complicity of local authority members in contractor conflicts for economic and political reasons, failure of early warning and prevention mechanisms regarding community-based violence; and also local residents claims that foreigners took jobs opportunities away from local south Africans and they accept lower wages, foreigners do not participate in the struggle for better wages and working conditions. Other local South Africans claim that foreigners are criminals, and they should not have access to services and police protection. Foreigners are also blamed for their businesses that take away customers from local residents and the spread of diseases such as HIV/AIDS. Other South African locals do not particularly like the presence of refugees, asylum-seekers or foreigners in their communities.

Cases of xenophobic attacks

In December 1994 and January 1995, armed youth gangs in the Alexandra Township outside of Johannesburg, Gauteng Province, destroyed the homes and property of suspected undocumented migrants and marched the individuals down to the local police station where they demanded that the foreigners be forcibly and immediately removed. In September 1998, two Senegalese and a Mozambican were thrown from a moving train in Johannesburg by a group of individuals returning from a rally organised by a group blaming foreigners for the levels of unemployment, crime, and even the spread of AIDS. In the township of Zandspruit, a township in of Johannesburg, residents went on a rampage burning down shacks of Zimbabwean foreigners living in the settlement with the intention of driving out foreigners they claimed were stealing their jobs and causing crime.

In 2000, seven xenophobic killings were reported in the Cape Flats district of Cape Town. Kenyan Kingori Siguri Joseph died in Tambo Close, Khanya Park in Gugulethu after being attacked and shot. In separate incidents, two Nigerians were shot dead in NY 99 in Gugulethu. Prince Anya, 36, who owned a restaurant in Sea Point, was hijacked with his wife Tjidi and their toddler in Adam Tas Road, Bothasig. In Mdolomda Street in Langa, two Angolan brothers were trapped inside their house and burnt to death. Nguiji Chicola, 23, and Mario Gomez Inacio, 25, were in their house when it was set alight by several men who then ran away. The brothers burnt to death.

On May 11 2008, an outburst of xenophobic violence in the Johannesburg Township Alexandra triggered more xenophobic violence in other townships. Firstly, it only spread in the Gauteng province. After two weeks, the violence spread to other urban areas across the country, mainly Durban and Cape Town. But it also emerged in townships in more rural areas such as Limpopo Province. The violence consisted of attacks both verbally and physically by inhabitants of the townships on other inhabitants. The victims were called foreigners, referring to their nationality being non-South African and predominantly Zimbabwean and Mozambican. As a result many houses were burnt, 342 shops were looted and 213 burnt down. Hundreds of people were injured, thousands chased away and the death toll after the attacks stood at 56.

Mozambican Ernesto Alfabeto Nhamuave, who was 35 years old, was beaten, stabbed and set alight in Ramaphosa informal settlement on the East Rand. Nobody had been arrested for his horrible murder. Police closed the case on 27 October 2010 after concluding that there were no witnesses and no suspects. In all, 62 people were killed. On 24 May 2008, Spaza shops owned by Pakistan, Somalis, and Ethiopians were attacked, their stocks were looted and the doors ripped down. The looting was widespread in Sebokeng, Orange Farm, and Evaton areas South of Johannesburg.

From 14 to 17 November 2009, 3000 Zimbabwean citizens living in the rural community of De Doorns, an informal settlement near Breede Valley Municipality, in the Western Cape was displaced as a result of xenophobic violence. It selectively targeted Zimbabweans despite the presence of other foreign nationals (e.g. Lesotho nationals) living and working in the same area. There had been destruction and looting of Zimbabweans dwellings by their South African neighbours.

Violence occurred in three informal settlements: Ekuphumleni, Stofland and Hasie Square located in Ward 2 of De Doorns, Breede Valley Municipality, Western Cape. The first wave of attacks took place on 14 November 20009 in Ekuphumleni, displacing 68 Zimbabwean nationals. On 17 November 2009, the violence intensified, spreading to Stofland and Hasie Square. This second wave displaced approximately 3000 Zimbabweans. While the displaced initially sought protection at the De Doorns police station, they were moved to a local sports field called Hexvallei Sportklub on 18 November 2009 as numbers increased. Shelter and humanitarian assistance were provided at the sports field.

On 27 February 2013, eight South African police officers tied the 27 years old Mozambican man, Mido Macia, to the back of a police van and dragged him down the road. Subsequently, the man died in a police cell from head injuries. The incident happened in Daveyton, East of Johannesburg, South Africa. On 26 May 2013, two Zimbabwean men were killed by South Africans mob in xenophobic violence in Diepsloot, South Africa.

In January 2015, a Somali shop owner shot and killed a 14-year-old boy, Siphiwe Mahori, during an alleged robbery in Soweto Township. The boy was shot in the neck and died within 15 minutes. Lebogang Ncamla, 23, was another victim when he was shot three times in the arm. The incident triggered waves of attacks and looting of foreign owned shops. An estimated 120 Spaza shops owned by Somalis and Bangladeshis across Snake Park, Zola, Meadowlands, Slovoville, Kagiso, Zondi and Emdeni in Soweto *were looted*. It was also reported that police actively stole goods and helped others raid the shops during the worst attacks on foreigners. In Zondi Section, the police instructed looters to queue outside a foreign-owned shop and allowed four of them in at a time to prevent a stampede. Police arrested a suspect accused of killed 14-year-old Mahori, along with a number of looters and foreign nationals for possessing three unlicensed firearms.

On 5 March 2015, xenophobic attacks occurred in Limpopo Province. Foreigners on the outskirts of Polokwane left their shops after protesting villagers threatened to burn them alive and then looted them. Violence erupted in the Ga-Sekgopo area after a foreign shop owner was found in possession of a mobile phone belonging to a local man who was killed. Villagers demanded answers as to how the shop owner got the killed man's phone. They didn't know whether it was sold to him or was brought there to be fixed. Violent protests erupted with villagers sending all the foreigners packing and pushing them out of 11 villages in Sekgopo. One of the shop owners reported loss of stock.

On 21 March 2015, Zulu King Goodwill Zwelithini made comments that foreigners should go back to their home countries because they are changing the nature of South African society with their goods and enjoying wealth that should have been for local people. This horrified foreigners who have been dealing with a spate of xenophobic attacks around the country. King Zwelithini made these comments at the moral regeneration event in Pongola, Kwazulu Natal Province. The king's statement came while Congolese nationals were mourning deaths caused by a series of xenophobic attacks. Noel Beya Dinshistia from Congo, a bouncer at a local nightclub, was doused in a flammable substance before being set alight while on duty two weeks ago.

On 8 April 2015, the spate of xenophobic violence increased. On 10 April 2015, two Ethiopian brothers were critically injured when their shop, in a shipping container, was set on fire while they were trapped inside. One of the men died while in hospital. The other is fighting for his life.

On 12 April 2015, Attacks on foreign nationals continued in KwaZulu-Natal when shops in Umlazi and KwaMashu, outside Durban, were torched. In V Section, a shop owned by a foreign national was set on fire by a mob of suspects. There was another fire which we believewas set by local people at a foreign-owned property in G Section. Almost 2,000 foreign nationals from Malawi, Zimbabwe, Mozambique and Burundi have been displaced as a result of the violence. Five people have been killed.

On 14 April 2015, Looting of foreign shops spread to Verulam, north of Durban following a day of clashes between locals, foreigners, and police in the city centre, KwaZulu-Natal. About 300 local people looted foreign-owned shops, and only two people have been arrested. A 14-year-old boy became the latest fatality. He was shot dead during looting in KwaNdlanzi, allegedly by two security guards. In Durban's Central Business District (CBD), a car was set alight and police fired rubber bullets, stun grenades and teargas canisters in clashes between looters and foreigners.

Four refugee camps have been set up by the KwaZulu-Natal provincial government to house the displaced foreigners who say they are destitute, with some saying they want to go home. At least 28 people were arrested on Sunday night during xenophobic violence in which Somali, Ethiopian and Pakistani people were attacked.

References

Carien, J. T. (2009). Ernesto Burning: an analyses of Dutch print media coverage on the 2008 xenophobic violence in South Africa. Available at: https://carienjtouwen.wordpress.com/essays/reporting-on-xenophobia-in-so... [accessed on 13 April 2015]

Cornish, Jean-Jacques. (2015). South Africa: Xenophobic Attacks Erupt in South Africa's Limpopo Province. Available at: http://allafrica.com/stories/201503051136.html [accessed on 14 April 2015]

IoL News. (2000). xenophobic attacks: seven die in one month. Available at: http://www.iol.co.za/news/south-africa/xenophobic-attacks-seven-die-in-one-month-1.45733#.VS4-LPCROYM [accessed on 15 April 2015]

Misago, J, P. (2009). Violence, labour and displacement of Zimbabweans in De Doorns, Western Cape. *Migration policy brief 2*. Forced migration studies programme, University of the Witwatersrand.

Nicolson, G and Simelane, BC. (2015). Xenophobia rears its head again: Looting, shooting, dying in Soweto. Available at: http://

www.dailymaverick.co.za/article/2015-01-22-xenophobia-rears-its-head-again-looting-shooting-dying-in-soweto/#.VS4eg_CROYM [accessed on 15 April 2015]

Valji, N. (2003). Creating the Nation: The rise of violent xenophobia in the New South Africa. Unpublished Masters Thesis, York University. Available at: http://csvr.org.za/old/docs/foreigners/riseofviolent.pdf [accessed on 14 April 2015]

Wicks, J. (2015). KZN xenophobic violence spreads to KwaMashu. Available at: http://www.news24.com/SouthAfrica/News/KZN-xenophobic-violence-spreads-to-KwaMashu-20150413 [accessed on 14 April 2015]

Hans, B. (2015). King's anti-foreigner speech causes alarm. Available at:http://www.iol.co.za/news/politics/king-s-anti-foreigner-speech-causes-alarm-1.1835602#.VSzaLPCROYM [accessed on 14 April 2015]

In the United States, Hate Crime Statistics Tell a Story of Their Own

William B. Rubenstein

In the following excerpted viewpoint, William Rubenstein, the Sidley Austin Professor of Law at Harvard Law School, argues that the reported number and types of hate crimes are often summarized and, therefore, do not reveal the truth. Rubenstein, who specializes in civil rights cases and advocating for the rights of LGBT+ citizens, claims that a more detailed analysis of the reports has much to offer, such as the identification of the source of the report—which also identifies a targeted population—and that there needs to be differentiation between groups within targeted populations.

As you read, consider the following questions:

1. What is the most frequently reported type of hate crime? Second most? Third?
2. Who files these reports?
3. How can reported statistics provide evidence to the rise in anti-Muslim hate crime?

"The Real Story of U.S. Hate Crimes Statistics: An Empirical Analysis," by William B. Rubenstein. Reprinted by Permission.

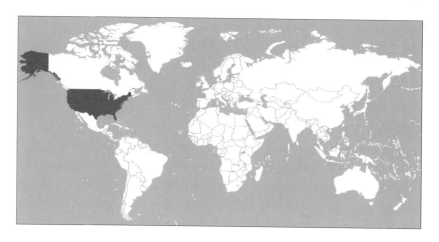

The Real Story of U.S. Hate Crimes Statistics: An Empirical Analysis

Introduction

For more than a decade, the federal government has collected and published data on hate crimes. At least since the mid-1990s, the number of hate crimes reported has been remarkably consistent: Each year, throughout the United States, there are about 4,600 reported incidents of racial hate crimes, 1,400 religious hate crimes, and 1,250 sexual orientation hate crimes. The story told about these numbers also has been remarkably consistent. Government officials, researchers, advocates, and the media all regularly announce that racial hate crimes are the most frequently reported, followed by religious hate crimes, and sexual orientation hate crimes.

As is evident from the numbers provided above, this "conventional story" is not, technically speaking, wrong. But it is neither the whole story that the data present, nor a particularly insightful one. There are at least three problems with this conventional account. First, the conventional story is told in the neutral language of American antidiscrimination discourse—"racial" hate crimes, or "sexual orientation" hate crimes. This language obscures the specific minority groups that are the actual targets of most hate crimes. Second, the hierarchy of hate crimes constituted by the conventional story fails to account for population disparities among the targeted groups: It expresses hate crime reports only in total counts and not on a per capita basis. Finally, the composite data mask important distinctions between crimes against property and crimes against people.

Taking each of these points in turn, I construct a different, more nuanced, story about the hate crimes data. The vast majority (about two-thirds) of racial hate crimes are reported by blacks; an overwhelming portion (about three-fourths) of the religious hate crimes are reported by Jewish people; and almost all of the sexual orientation hate crimes are reported by gay people. What's more, two of these groups, Jewish people and gay people, constitute a remarkably small portion of the total population. When the data are adjusted for the prevalence of a group in the population, they suggest that gay people report hate crimes at per capita rates that are higher than any other group, followed by Jewish people and blacks. Per capita, these three groups' hate crime reports far exceed the reporting rates of other groups. These two points alone comprise a new story.

But even that new story has another twist. A significant proportion of the anti-Semitic hate crimes are property-related, typically hate crimes defiling synagogues or cemeteries. Per capita, Jewish "places" report hate crimes more often than any other covered group's places. Yet what this also means is that if property crimes are extracted from the per capita counts, the chances that a gay person's body will be the subject of a hate crime report become even that much greater, indeed remarkably greater than the risks faced—at least before September 11, 2001—by any other group.

This Article provides a statistical demonstration of this new story. In so doing, the Article also provides a new context in which to analyze the post-September 11 rise in hate crimes against Muslims and Arabs. Currently, federal data are only available through the end of 2001. These data provide some sense of the remarkable spike in these hate crimes in the immediate aftermath of September 11.

And placed in population context, the data show that Arabs in America reported hate crimes in late 2001 at rates similar to, or beyond those, of the regular reporting rates of the gay and Jewish populations. Standing alone, however, the 2001 data do not enable an evaluation of whether this was a momentary spike, or a new form of recurring hate crime. Nonetheless, this Article's empirical analysis of hate crimes helps provide a needed framework—never provided in general media accounts—in which to consider the post-September 11th anti-Arab hate crime epidemic.

Finally, by unveiling the real story behind the hate crimes statistics, this Article answers the call Congress issued when it authorized the federal government to collect hate crimes statistics. Congress specifically asserted that these data would help frame future legislative action. Now that the data demonstrate which groups are most likely to report hate crimes, Congress has a special responsibility to act so as to ensure protection for these groups. This is especially true in the case of gay people, who are not currently protected against discrimination by federal law.

Hate Crimes and Hate Crime Statistics

Hate crimes refer to criminal acts that are motivated by particular types of bias or prejudice. Although age old, hate crimes have developed as a special category of American criminal law in the past quarter century. Most states have adopted laws explicitly criminalizing hate crimes or enhancing penalties for underlying crimes where bias is a motivating factor (or both).

Congress entered the field with its 1990 adoption of the Hate Crimes Statistics Act (HCSA). HCSA seeks to "address heightened concern over the bias crime problem," but does so only by attempting "to provide trustworthy statistics for bias crime observers." HCSA defines hate crimes in terms of twelve predicate offenses and five types of bias. HCSA neither criminalizes hate crimes nor enhances penalties for them (though a later federal law does provide for enhanced penalties). HCSA simply requires the Justice Department to collect information about hate crimes as part of its regular information-gathering function. The Justice Department's data, collected by the Federal Bureau of Investigation (FBI) through the Uniform Crime Reporting Program (UCRP), nonetheless provide a unique resource for investigating the nature and prevalence of bias crimes.

Yet, as is evident, the Justice Department's data collection and publication efforts arose in the context of a limited, federal criminal regime. Not surprisingly, these efforts were launched rather slowly and remain widely criticized for a number of reasons. To understand the limitations of this reporting regime, it is helpful to follow a hate crime from commission to the possibility of its appearance in the Uniform Crime Report (UCR). First, HCSA covers only a limited number of crimes and biases. Thus a hate crime perpetuated on the basis of sexual orientation, but taking the form of blackmail, would not be a HCSA-covered crime. Relatedly, the murder of a union organizer would not fall within the categories of prohibited bias. Second, even if a HCSA-covered crime is committed, the victim must report the crime. There are a variety of reasons that hate crime victims might not report. An individual who is assaulted upon leaving a gay bar, for example, might worry that reporting the crime will bring unwanted public attention to his or her sexual orientation, or that police officers to whom the crime is reported may be unsympathetic, or that a jury is ultimately unlikely to convict the defendant in a gay-related assault. Similarly, people of color may significantly distrust the police and be hesitant to report hate crimes for that reason.

Third, assuming a hate crime covered by HCSA is reported, the police must nonetheless characterize the crime as such. There are a number of reasons that the police might not do so. For starters, a state might have a legal regime that covers hate crimes in different ways than HCSA, so the police might want to avoid the complexities involved even in merely reporting a hate crime. Categorizing a crime as a hate crime also requires additional investigation to prove the hate-based nature of the crime. Such an investigation might not be one that the police are well-trained to undertake nor one upon which they particularly want to expend resources. Moreover, police officers might be hesitant to acknowledge the existence of bias, in addition to crime, in their precincts. Fourth, even if a hate crime is covered, reported, and classified by the local law enforcement agency, it must nonetheless be reported to the FBI to show up in the UCR. HCSA does not require local law enforcement officers to report data to the FBI nor provide funding to assist in the effort. Local jurisdictions have been lax in doing so, perhaps, again, for either resource or reputational reasons. Even where jurisdictions have reported to HCSA, the data they report tend to be significantly less than the data collected by advocacy groups in the same geographical location for the same years.

All of these problems with HCSA limit the usefulness of the resulting UCR data. Researchers cannot, for example, make reliable estimates of temporal trends nor easily compare different jurisdictions to one another. Despite these limitations, the UCR data are "the most comprehensive and representative data currently available." To date, scholars have undertaken only a few limited analyses of the data. Most often, the data are used simply to support the recurring claim that racial hate crimes constitute the largest number of such crimes each year, followed by religious hate crimes and sexual orientation hate crimes. The FBI, advocates, law professors, law students, and the media all report this. These reports tend not to break down the categories into particular groups, nor adjust reporting data for population size, nor probe distinctions between property and personal crimes.

In America, Negative Attitudes Toward Muslim Americans Post-9/11 Are Varied

Mussarat Khan and Kathryn Ecklund

In the following viewpoint, authors Khan and Ecklund argue that since the terrorist attacks on September 11, 2001, anti-Muslim attitudes in America have skyrocketed. Surprisingly, they claim that anti-Muslim sentiments voiced by non-Muslims are not generalized but are, rather, based on specific situations, such as Muslims boarding a plane or selling a used car. They base their claims on a social desirability study they conducted among psychology students at a California State University campus. Mussarat Khan has been affiliated with Alliant University in California; Kathryn Ecklund is chair and professor of psychology at Azusa Pacific University, also in California.

As you read, consider the following questions:

1. What was the increase in reported hate crimes against Muslim-Americans in the year prior to the 9/11 attacks?
2. What kind of a label is "Muslim?"
3. What is social desirability?

"Attitudes Toward Muslim Americans Post-9/11," by Mussarat Khan and Kathryn Ecklund. Michigan State University, 2012. Reprinted by permission of the author.

Abstract

Attitudes toward Muslim Americans have been largely understudied in the psychological field. It is important to identify negative attitudes that may be present in particular situations for Muslim Americans in order to better understand and adapt to situations in which negative attitudes are expressed. For this study, 208 subjects (170 females and 38 males) from a California State University campus were recruited; the study explored situational attitudes toward Muslim Americans within the context of social desireability and universal orientation. Contrary to expectations, negative attitudes appeared to be specific rather than global. Implications of the study findings for Muslim American mental health and prevention/intervention programs are discussed.

Attitudes Toward Muslim Americans Post-9/11

Following September 11, 2001, the Federal Bureau of Investigation (FBI) reported a 1,700 percent increase of hate crimes against Muslim Americans between 2000 to 2001 (Anderson, 2002). During the process of adjusting to the aftermath of September 11, Muslim Americans faced an upsurge in negative stereotypes expressed by the larger society (American-Arab Anti-Discrimination Committee, 2003; Cassel, 2006) and Muslim immigrants, more than any other immigrant group, were met with negative attitudes

(Council of American Islamic Relations, 2003; Saroglou & Galand, 2004). Since then, increased racial and religious animosity has left Arabs, Middle Easterners, Muslims, and those who bear stereotyped physical resemblance to members of these groups, fearful of potential hatred and hostility from persons of other cultures (Abu-Ras & Suarez, 2009; Baqi-Aziz, 2001; Kira et al., 2010; Rippy & Newman, 2006).

Although Muslim is a religious label and does not pertain to race, the line between racism and religious discrimination is often blurred (Allen & Nielsen, 2002). Muslim Americans are often perceived as a monolithic group (McCarus, 1994; Nyang, 1999), conceptualized as a religious minority thought to act, think, and behave similarly despite wide ethnic differences that exist within the Muslim American community (Abu-Ras & Suarez, 2009; McCarus, 1994; Pew Research Center, 2010).

Despite negative stereotypes of Muslims reported in the media, little psychological research has been conducted to characterize non-Muslim attitudes toward Muslim Americans. One study was published exploring negative attitudes toward Arabs, whereas none has been conducted regarding Muslims (Sergent, Woods, & Sedlacek, 1992). Research focusing on Islamophobia, a dread or hatred of Islam, has been conducted in Europe where a survey in the United Kingdom indicated that discrimination against Muslims has increased in recent years (Sheridan, 2006).

As many Muslim Americans are visibly culturally distinct, it would be of value to explore whether attitudes of non-Muslims toward Muslim Americans resemble attitudes expressed by European non-Muslims toward members of these minority groups. In the aftermath of September 11, because of the higher occurrences of discriminating incidents directed toward Muslims and those perceived to be Muslims (Sheridan, 2006), it is important to identify the particular situational contexts in which Muslim Americans are most vulnerable to experiences of expressed negative attitudes toward their self or their cultural group. Such information may help Muslim Americans process and understand negative experiences through the lens of racism and racism inoculation (Comas-Diaz & Jacobsen, 2001). The present study explores situational attitudes toward Muslim Americans. We examine negative attitudes that may be present toward Muslim Americans which may have detrimental effects on the Muslim American's experiences in specific contexts.

It has been established that discrimination toward Muslim Americans was present before the attacks on September 11, which may relate to Islam being frequently portrayed by the media as intrinsically intolerant and violent (Giger & Davidhizar, 2002). However, it would be beneficial to study situational attitudes toward Muslim Americans post-September 11, 2001, as the attacks by Muslim terrorists seemed to worsen the general public's attitudes toward mainstream Muslim Americans. Since Muslim Americans are part of American society, negative attitudes and discrimination would have detrimental effects not only on the recipients of the negative expression (Abu-Ras & Suarez, 2009: Rippy & Newman, 2006; Kira et al., 2010), but also on society at large. Greater understanding of non-Muslims' affective response to Muslims might be useful information to guide efforts to reduce prejudice toward this group. However, the effects of situational factors on attitudes toward Muslim Americans in the aftermath of September 11, 2001 have not been directly examined. In the present study, we explore the type of situation-specific attitudes held by undergraduate non-Muslim students toward Muslim Americans post-September 11, 2001.

To be able to assess an individual's affect toward a particular situation, it is important to understand the role of social desirability. Social desirability bias is "the tendency for individuals to portray themselves in a generally favorable fashion" (Rudmin, 1999, p. 229). The tendency for an individual to do this varies and may depend on the context. It becomes important to measure social desirability bias when using various self-report questionnaires in social, clinical, and personality psychology research (Rudmin, 1999). Typically, social desirability bias has been assumed to be a function of two factors- first, the general strength for the need of approval by others, and second, the demands of the particular situation (Phillips & Clancy, 1970). The overreporting of socially desirable behaviors and the underreporting of socially undesirable behaviors becomes problematic when researching sensitive attitudes. Social desirability bias can attenuate, inflate, or moderate the relationships found between variables (Fischer & Fick, 1993). In relation to attitudes toward Muslim Americans, one would assume if a person is high on traits of social desirability he may minimize negative attitudes held toward Muslim Americans.

Furthermore, when considering attitudes toward Muslim Americans, it is important to consider if respondents' worldview is non-prejudicial. Allport, in his theory of universal orientation, argued people have a "slant, a directional set, a posture, to the mind" that begins the process of selective perception (Allport, 1954; as cited in Phillips & Ziller, 1997). Universal orientation describes the process by which one integrates perceptual data into a sense of oneself and others (Phillips & Ziller, 1997). According to this theory, a person, depending on their orientation, attends to an array of potentially colliding stimuli and focuses on information that reinforces her original view of self or other. Hence, as cited in Phillips & Ziller (1997) "orientation is one of the earliest processes in the perceptual-cognitive sequence and is an interactive feature of a perceiver's personality that allows the actor to actively construe a supporting social niche for the self" (pp. 421–422). Therefore, universal orientation is characterized by a "slant, set, perceptual readiness" or a customary orientation toward finding and attending to similarities between self and others. Using this model, we argue that persons with non-prejudiced orientations toward others are more likely to respond with more positive attitudes toward Muslim Americans due to a genuine tendency to emphasize universal commonalities.

The present study is designed to examine the following hypotheses:

- Participants responding to various specific situations in which a Muslim American is present will evaluate those situations more negatively than participants evaluating a situation in which the party or parties are not given a specific Muslim American ethnic designation.

- Respondents who demonstrate high social desirability and nonprejudicial orientation will express more positive attitudes toward Muslim Americans.

Method

Participants

Participants were recruited from the psychology subject pool at California State University, Sacramento. Participants did not receive any monetary gain for completing the study, however, students at this university are required to participate in research studies as part of their studies in psychology. The inclusion criteria consisted of students who were currently enrolled in psychology classes at the university.

A total of 208 subjects (170 females and 38 males) participated in this study. Among the participants, 36.5% were Caucasian/European American, 25% were Asian/Pacific Islander, 13.5% were Hispanic/Latino, 8.2% were Black/African American, 3% were Middle Eastern, and 32% were "other" or unidentified ethnic origin. The participant's ages ranged from 18 to 49 years old with a median age of 21 years old. Of the 208 participants, 36.1% were Catholic, 29.3% were Christian, 4.8% were Buddhist, 1.9% were Muslim, 1.9% were Atheist, 1.4% were Jewish, 1% were Hindu, 10.1% were "other, and 13.5% reported "none" for religious affiliation. Muslim American and Middle Easterner participants were excluded from analysis. The remaining 204 participants were included in analyses.

Materials

Situational Attitude Scale

Participants were given the Situational Attitude Scale (SAS). Sedlacek and Brooks (1970) developed the Situational Attitude Scale (SAS) to assess if a given group may experience negative attitudes by others. The SAS is composed of ten personal and social situations followed by ten bipolar semantic differential scales. Two versions are utilized, one that is ethnic specific (in this study, Muslim American) and one that does not designate ethnicity. Reliabilities for each situational scale have been reported to range from alpha coefficients of .71 to .91, with a median of .84 (Sergent, Woods, & Sedlacek, 1992).

The SAS has been used to assess attitudes toward various racial, cultural, and ethnic groups. For example, groups such as African Americans (Balenger, Hoffman, & Sedlacek, 1992), Hispanics (White & Sedlacek, 1987), American Indians (Ancis, Choney, & Sedlacek, 1996), Asian Americans (Leong & Schneller, 1997), persons with disabilities (McQuilkin, Freitag, & Harris, 1990), women (Minatoya & Sedlacek, 1983), Arab Americans (Sergent, Woods, & Sedlacek, 1992) and Jews (Gerson & Sedlacek, 1992) have been studied using variations in which the appropriate ethnic term is used in ethnic specific form.

In this study, the situations utilized with the SAS were adopted from the study conducted by Sergent, Woods, and Sedlacek (1992) regarding attitudes toward Arabs. However, this study used "Muslim Americans" rather than "Arabs" to encompass all ethnicities that regard themselves as Muslims. The 10 situations utilized in this study are listed in table 1.

Marlowe-Crowne Social Desirability Scale

The Marlowe-Crowne Social Desirability Scale (MCSD) was developed to measure if "bias towards affirming social norms" is present in respondents (Rudmin, 1999). The MCSD scale is one of the oldest and most widely used scales measuring social desirability (Crown & Marlowe, 1964). The scale consists of 33 positively and negatively keyed items to which respondents can respond "true" or "false". Individuals whose responses to this scale are more socially desirable are thought to be more "conforming, cautious, and persuadable, and their behavior is more normatively anchored than persons who depict themselves less euphemistically" (Crowne & Marlowe, 1964, p. 189). The authors reported obtaining a Kuder-

Richardson reliability coefficient of .88 and a test-retest correlation of .89 (Leite & Beretvas, 2005).

Universal Orientation Scale

The Universal Orientation Scale (UOS) was developed by Phillips and Ziller in 1997. This measurement consists of 20 positively and negatively keyed items involving a 5-point Likert rating scale. Universal orientation theory posits that some individuals attenuate and emphasize self-other similarities resulting in integration of self and others. The importance of measuring nonprejudiced thinking is based on the idea that intergroup thinking is crucial for improving intergroup relations (Brown, Boniecki, & Walters, 2004).

Respondents with higher scores on the UOS are more accepting and less discriminating between minority and nonminority control targets, are concerned about the value of human equality, and are more willing to interact with a wide range of others (Phillips & Ziller, 1997). The scale has a moderate reliability of .75 and alpha coefficient of .76 (Nicol & Boies, 2006). Additionally, the UOS has been reported to be uncorrelated (-.05) with the Marlowe-Crowne Social Desirability Scale (Bringle, Phillips, & Hudson, 2004).

Procedure

Participants were asked to sign up for a time slot to complete this study on the research website for the psychology department. Participants attended their assigned time and independently completed the survey in a laboratory setting in groups of eight.

Two versions of the survey packets were constructed. These packets were identical in content, with the exception of the SAS, where each packet contained either Situational Attitude Scale (SAS) ethnic specific (Muslim American) form or SAS ethnicity not specified form. Both packets contained the demographic questionnaire, the Marlow-Crowne Social Desirability Scale (MCSD) and the Universal Orientation Scale (UOS). Packets were randomly distributed to participants. Each participant had an equal chance of receiving either version. Participants were unaware that two different versions of the packets existed.

Results

Data coding and preliminary analyses

The Situational Attitude Scale (SAS) was coded according to the direction of the attitude toward each situation. Each situation included ten bipolar semantic differential scales that were coded with higher scores indicating more negative attitudes. For the Marlowe-Crowne Social Desirability Scale (MCSD), the negatively keyed items were reverse coded as directed by the author (Crowne & Marlowe, 1964); with higher scores indicating more socially desirable responses. Negatively keyed items on the Universal Orientation Scale (UOS) were also reverse coded as indicated by the authors Phillips and Ziller (1997). Higher scores on the UOS indicated higher nonprejudiced thought.

On the SAS, mean scores were computed for each situation across the ten items pertaining to that situation. To reduce the number of potential dependent variables, a principal component analysis was conducted using the mean scores for the ten different situations of the SAS. Two factors had Eigenvalues greater than 1—all situations except seven and situation seven by itself. Together these two factors accounted for 49.90 % of the variance.

[...]

Attitudes toward Muslim American
versus unspecified ethnicity

The first hypothesis suggested that attitudes toward Muslim American individuals would be more negative than attitudes toward individuals of unspecified ethnicity in specific contexts. To assess this hypothesis, the average attitude scores for each situation were entered as dependent variable into separate one-way between-subjects analysis of variances (ANOVAs) with form type as the independent variable. The results indicated that in three of the ten situations, attitude scores were significantly different toward the Muslim American individual versus the individual of unspecified ethnicity. These included situation one, "You are standing on a very crowded bus surrounded by many (Muslim American) people"; situation three, "You are boarding a plane for a vacation in Florida, and two young (Muslim American) men are boarding immediately behind you"; and situation four, "You are buying a used car from a (Muslim American) salesman." Attitudes toward Muslim Americans were more negative in the plane and buying a used car but more positive in the crowded bus situation.

Pearson correlations were conducted to examine if there were any relations between attitudes toward Muslim Americans in situations one, three, and four and the UOS and MCSD. The MCSD negatively correlated with attitudes in situation one (bus) and situation three (plane); indicating respondents who had higher socially desirable responses also expressed more positive attitudes toward Muslim Americans in these situations. An analysis of covariance (ANCOVA) testing attitude differences toward Muslim Americans versus unspecified individuals was significant when MCSD was entered as a covariate for situation one, $F (1, 102) = 7.42$, $p < .01$, and situation three, $F (1, 102) = 14.52$, $p < .001$, indicating more negative attitudes toward Muslim Americans in the plane situation and more positive attitudes toward Muslim Americans in the bus situation could not be fully explained by social desirability.

Attitudes were also analyzed using the general situational attitude mean score averaged over the nine questions. A one-way between-subjects ANOVA revealed no significant difference between attitudes expressed toward Muslim Americans and attitudes toward individuals of unspecified ethnicity, $F(1, 202) < 1$.

Predicting attitudes toward Muslim Americans

The second hypothesis indicated individuals expressing nonprejudiced universal orientation would overall have more positive attitudes toward Muslim Americans. Additionally, it was hypothesized that individuals with higher socially desirable responses would have more positive responses toward Muslim Americans.

Pearson correlations of demographic data with the SAS scores revealed four relevant factors (age, gender, generational status, and race). These factors were utilized with the UOS and MCSD as independent variables in a standard multiple regression analysis. The analysis examined the relationships between the six independent variables and the general situational attitudes toward Muslim Americans across the nine situations. The regression model was significant, $F(6, 88) = 3.43$, $p < .05$. The regression model included one significant predictor; MCSD responses. High MCSD scores predicted less negative attitudes toward Muslim Americans. The regression model explained 19% of the variance. A similar standard multiple regression analysis predicting negative attitude in the cheating situation produced a model that included two significant predictors: age and if participant was born in the United States. The model was significant $F(6, 88) = 3.10$, $p < .05$, and explained 17% of the variance; indicating older and US-born participants expressed more negative attitudes toward the Muslim American individual in the cheating situation.

Discussion

A major goal of this study was to examine if attitudes toward Muslim Americans were in fact more negative than attitudes expressed toward individuals whose ethnicities were unspecified. It was hypothesized that attitudes would be more negative in instances where a Muslim American was identified versus instances where the ethnicity of the individual was unspecified. Rather than global negative attitudes, we found more negative attitudes to be present in specific situational contexts; specifically when Muslim Americans were boarding a plane to Florida or selling a used car. Additionally, older and US-born participants appeared to have more negative attitudes toward a Muslim American cheating on an exam. However, attitudes toward Muslim Americans appeared to be more positive than those toward nonspecified group members in the context of a crowded bus situation. These results were not expected.

It was hypothesized that participants who scored higher on the social desirability scale and the scale of nonprejudice would report more positive situational attitudes toward Muslim Americans. As predicted, findings indicated social desirability predicted higher expression of positive attitudes toward Muslim Americans; however, nonprejudiced universal orientation was not found to be related to attitudes toward Muslims. When social desirability was covaried, significant differences between attitudes toward Muslim American versus unspecified individuals still existed, indicating results could not be explained solely by social desirability for the presence of positive attitudes in situation one (bus) and negative attitudes in situation three (plane).

Our findings did not support the hypothesis that attitudes toward Muslim Americans would be more negative overall. Significant differences were not found in all situations. These findings may suggest attitudes toward Muslim Americans may be situationally variant.

Specific versus global attitudes

In situations where Muslim Americans were boarding a plane, higher negative attitudes were present. In light of the September 11 events, negative attitudes in plane situations might be expected more than negative attitudes in other situations. Specifically, individuals may express fear related to being on an airplane with a Muslim American. However, individuals did not express negative attitudes toward Muslim Americans in most other situations.

Research indicates that situations that are most salient in individuals' cognition tend to be more accessible. Due to the saliency of the traumatic events of September 11, generalizing the terrorists of 9/11 to all Muslims could possibly explain the presence of these negative attitudes. Evidence for this is found in reports that directly after September 11, individuals identified to be Muslim in Europe were targeted and attacked because they were perceived to be associated with the terrorist acts (Sheridan, 2006). However, the presence of negative attitudes may represent an intensification of preexisting attitudes toward Muslim Americans rather than signifying a new problem (Sheridan, 2006).

Additionally, due to the length of time between this study and the events of September 11, and the daily exposure of news content being lessened (Persson & Musher-Eizenman, 2005), there are several possible explanations for this pattern of small to moderate effect. Consistent with the accessibility principle, it is possible the higher amounts of media coverage immediately after the attacks presented vast amounts of negative images related to Muslims and Arabs in general, thus leading to greater but temporary prejudices toward this group (CAIR, 2001). Furthermore, some research has indicated that manipulating the salience of people's own death alters attitudes toward out-group members (Persson & Musher-Eizenman, 2005). Perhaps images of victims and death broadcast following the terrorist attacks exacerbated viewers' negative attitudes toward Muslim Americans (Persson & Musher-Eizenman, 2005).

Other research has indicated Americans possess a lingering resentment toward Arabs and Muslims in America post-September 11, as examined by opinion poll articles in the *Washington Post* (Panagopoulos, 2006). However, results of this study indicated people may feel negative in situations where they are more likely to feel threatened rather than holding negative attitudes overall toward this group. Thus, findings indicated negative attitudes are situation specific rather than global.

Role of social desirability

In line with the initial prediction, results indicated a positive relation between higher social desirability scores and higher positive attitudes toward Muslim Americans. In other words, the data indicated the need for individuals to portray themselves favorably is related to positive attitudes expressed toward Muslim Americans; possibly indicating attitudes toward Muslim Americans are in fact worse than indicated by the data. Additionally, results indicated positive attitudes toward Muslim Americans in the bus and negative attitudes toward the airplane situation could not be fully explained by social desirability. Findings of relatively positive attitudes toward Muslim Americans in the bus situation may indicate a perception of stereotypes that Muslim Americans are quiet, polite, and unobtrusive. Because these findings are counter to hypotheses, they should be replicated in future studies before placing a great deal of confidence in them.

It is also possible that people hold ambivalent feelings toward Muslim Americans. Due to both negative and positive experiences with this group, individuals may respond positively in some situations (such as the bus situation) and respond more negatively in other situations (such as airport situation). The presence of both these feelings and attitudes may not be a contradiction of each other; rather, it may explain the impact of the direct or indirect experiences of September 11.

Limitations and generalizations

Regarding methods of this study, possible improvements include examining a larger and broader participant population. The California State University at Sacramento campus represents one of the largest diverse college campuses in California. The city of Sacramento includes 41% of non-Hispanic whites, 15.5% of blacks, 22% of Hispanics, and 17.5% of Asians/Pacific Islanders (Stodghill & Bower, 2002), possibly indicating students at this campus have a higher awareness of diversity and have had prior interactions with Muslim Americans. This exposure to other cultures and Muslim Americans may have contributed to this population being more culturally aware and/or sensitive. Additionally, due to assessing student attitudes in an educational setting, results may not generalize to employment or other social settings, as college students may express more inclusive attitudes than the general population.

Alternative situational contexts could have been measured, as the ten situations utilized do not represent the range of intercultural interactions among Muslim Americans and non-Muslims. An additional limitation of this study included a higher rate of female subjects and subjects being limited to college students in psychology classes.

Future Research

The results of the current study point the way to future research. Future research exploring attitudes toward Muslim Americans may benefit from expanding the participant pool into communities that are less ethnically diverse, sociopolitically liberal, and highly educated. The current study utilized participants from a highly diverse university setting in a highly diverse, sociopolitically liberal community in a liberal state. Therefore, the current study may not represent the attitudes of students or others from less diverse or more conservative contexts. For example, a recent Pew opinion poll (Pew, 2010) found that Republicans express an unfavorable opinion of Islam two times higher than Democrats, and that college graduates report a 19% more positive view of Islam than those who have not graduated from college.

Future research may benefit from assessing factors that may contribute to positive or negative attitudes in non-Muslim individuals. The recent Pew opinion poll (2010) considered such factors as age, education, political affiliation, and familiarity with Islam. Additional factors such as ethnic identity, cultural mindedness/racism, religious identity salience, political awareness/ involvement, and socioeconomic status may play important roles in identifying and understanding the factors that contribute to attitudes toward Muslims. This research may help elucidate the findings of this study where college students reported negative attitudes toward Muslims boarding planes, but positive attitudes on a bus.

Future research may also explore whether people make distinctions between Muslim Americans and Muslims from other countries. It would be helpful to explore whether situational contexts in which negative attitudes are expressed toward Muslim Americans remain stable over time or whether they change with political conditions and public exposure.

Finally, possible follow-up studies can explore the influence of media exposure in positive and negative attitude toward Muslim Americans.

Further implications

The findings of this study suggest that there are likely specific situational contexts in which negative attitudes are more likely to be expressed. The findings of negative attitudes in airport situations points to the need for continuing efforts at public education regarding the diversity of Muslims and the nature of Islam and its beliefs. Understanding that expressed bias is linked to specific contexts can be useful in planning programs to help combat prejudicial attitudes and develop tolerance.

For example, rather than focusing on general attitudes toward Muslim Americans, which most non-Muslims would likely report as generally positive, anti-discrimination programs may benefit from identifying the common specific contexts in which negative bias is expressed. Then, as situation-specific biases are identified, tolerance programming may consider utilizing the social desirability tendency to engage non-Muslims in combating their own biases. Raising awareness of these biases in people with high social desirability tendencies will likely produce motivation to combat their internal biases. Relying on the findings that perception of threat to safety impacts salience of negative attitudes toward out-group members (Persson & Musher-Eizenman, 2005), anti-bias programs may consider including data based educational content. Specifically educating non-Muslims with information and objective data regarding safety and low probability of harm. Anti-bias programs may then coach non-Muslims to utilize the data for cognitive mediation of anxiety. Lowered anxiety, in turn, may assist in decreasing bias.

It appears that the U.S. population reports less generalized bias toward Muslim Americans than expected, and therefore, anti-discrimination programs may benefit from identifying salient situation specific settings in which bias is more likely to be acknowledged, and target psychoeducation and training toward these more specific and contextualized awareness.

Additionally, in relation to Muslim Americans, these findings suggest, as indicated by the Pew study (2010), Americans appear to be conflicted in their orientation toward Muslim Americans and Islam. Therefore, Muslim individual self report of anxiety resulting from unpredictability of negative sentiment toward Muslims (e.g., experiences with discrimination or racism) should be validated. Mental health prevention/intervention programs should consider psychoeducational strategies that validate such cognitive/affective experiences and provide coping strategies for management of anticipation anxiety and discrimination trauma (Rippy & Newman, 2006; Kira et al., 2010).

Muslim Americans who experience daily life interactions with non-Muslims as generally positive may experience a greater internal reaction to the periodic negative experience. Utilizing the concept of racism inoculation (Comas-Diaz & Jacobsen, 2001) in mental health intervention/prevention programs may be beneficial to Muslim Americans. As research findings better clarify the contextual variables that contribute to negative attitudes toward Muslim-Americans, the information should be incorporated into programs to aid Muslim Americans in understanding of the contexts in which non-Muslims are likely to possess negative attitudes toward Muslims. This will better prepare Muslims to process, engage in meaning-making, and, specifically, depersonalize these negative experiences.

References

Abu-Ras, W. M., & Suarez, Z. E. (2009). Muslim men and women's perception of discrimination, hate crimes, and PTSD symptoms post 9/11. *Traumatology, 15,* 48–63.

Allen, C., & Nielsen, J. S. (2002). *Summary report on Islamaphobia in the EU after 11 September 2001.* Vienna: European Monitoring Center on Racism and Xenophobia.

American-Arab Anti-Discrimination Committee. (2003). *Report on hate crimes and discrimination against Arab Americans: The post-September 11 backlash, September 11, 2001-October 11, 2002.* Washington, DC: American-Arab Anti-Discrimination Committee Research Institute.

Ancis, J. R., Choney, S. K., & Sedlacek, W. E. (1996). University student attitudes toward American Indians. *Journal of Multicultural Counseling and Development, 24,* 26–36.

Anderson, C. (2002, November 25). FBI reports jump in violence against Muslims. *Associated Press.*

Baqi-Aziz, M. A. (2001). 'Where does she think she is?': On being Muslim, an American, and a nurse. *American Journal of Nursing, 101,* 11–12.

Balenger, V. J., Hoffman, M. A., & Sedlacek, W. E. (1992). Racial attitudes among incoming White students: A study of 10-year trends. *Journal of College Student Development, 33,* 245–252.

Bringle, R. G., Phillips, M. A., & Hudson, M. (2004). *The measure of service learning: Research scales to assess student experiences.* Washington, DC: American Psychological Association.

Brown, L. M., Boniecki, K. A., & Walters, A. M. (2004). Intergroup flexibility and people's view of African Americans. *International Journal of Intercultural Relations, 28,* 373–398.

Comas-Diaz, L., & Jacobsen, F. M. (2001). Ethnocultural allodynia. *Journal of Psychotherapy Practice and Research, 10,* 246–252.

Council on American-Islamic Relations [CAIR]. (2001). *American Muslims: Population statistics.* Washington, DC: Council on American-Islamic Relations Research Center.

Crowne, D. P., & Marlowe, D. (1964). *The approval motive; studies in evaluative dependence.* New York: Wiley.

Fischer, D. G., & Fick, C. (1993). Measuring social desirability: Short forms of the Marlowe-Crowne Social Desirability Scale. *Educational and Psychological Measurement, 53,* 417–424.

Gerson, S. S., & Sedlacek, W. E. (1992). Student attitudes toward "JAPS": The new anti-semitism. *College Student Affairs Journal, 11*(3), 44–53.

Giger, J. N., & Davidhizar, R. (2002). Culturally competent care: Emphasis on understanding the people of Afghanistan, Afghanistan Americans, and Islamic culture and religion. *International Nursing Review, 49,* 79–86.

Kira, I. A., Lewandowski, L., Templin, T., Ramaswamy, V., Ozkan, B., & Mohanesh, J. (2010). The effects of perceived discrimination and backlash on Iraqi refugees' mental and physical health. *Journal of Muslim Mental Health, 5,* 59–81.

Leite, W. L., & Beretvas, S. N. (2005). Validation of scores on the Marlowe-Crowne Social Desirability Scale and the Balanced Inventory of Desirable Responding. *Educational and Psychological Measurement, 65,* 140–154.

Leong, F. T. L., & Schneller, G. (1997). White Americans' attitudes toward Asian Americans in social situations: An empirical examination of potential stereotypes, bias, and prejudice. *Journal of Multicultural Counseling and Development, 25,* 68–78.

McCarus, E. (Ed.). (1994). *The development of Arab-American identity.* Ann Arbor, MI: University of Michigan Press.

McQuilkin, J. I., Freitag, C. B., & Harris, J. L. (1990). Attitudes of college students toward handicapped persons. *Journal of College Student Development, 31,* 17–22.

Minatoya, L. Y., & Sedlacek, W. E. (1983). The Situational Attitude Scale toward women (SASW): A means to measure environmental sexism. *Journal of the National Association for Women Deans, Administrators, and Counselors, 47,* 26–30.

Nicol, A. M. & Boies, K. (2006). Evidence of reliability and validity for the Universal Orientation Scale. *Psychological Reports, 99,* 930–932.

Nyang, S. S. (1999). *Islam in the United States of America.* Chicago: ABC International Group, Inc.

Panagopoulos, C. (2006). The polls-trends: Arab and Muslim Americans and Islam in the aftermath of 9/11. *Public Opinion Quarterly, 70,* 608–624.

Persson, A. V., & Musher-Eizenman, D. R. (2005). College students' attitudes toward Blacks and Arabs following a terrorist attack as a function of varying levels of media exposure. *Journal of Applied Social Psychology, 35,* 1879–1892.

Pew Research Center (2010, August). Public remains conflicted over Islam. *The Pew Research Center For The People and The Press. Retrieved from*:http://pewresearch.org/pubs/1706/poll-americans-views-of-muslims-object-to-new-york-islamic-center-islam-violence.

Phillips, D. L., & Clancy, K. J. (1970). Responses biases in field studies of mental illness. *American Sociological Review, 35,* 503–515.

Phillips, S. T., & Ziller, R. C. (1997). Toward a theory and measure of the nature of nonprejudice. *Journal of Personality and Social Psychology, 72,* 420–434.

Rippy, A. E., & Newman, E. (2006). Perceived religious discrimination and its relationship to anxiety and paranoia among Muslim Americans. *Journal of Muslim Mental Health, 1,* 5–20.

Rudmin, F. W. (1999). Norwegian short-form of the Marlowe-Crowne Social Desirability Scale. *Scandinavian Journal of Psychology, 40,* 229-233.

Saroglou, V., & Galand, P. (2004). Identities, values, and religion: A study among Muslim, other immigrant, and native Belgian young adults after the 9/11 attacks. *Identity, 4*(2), 97–132.

Sedlacek, W. E., & Brooks, G. C., Jr. (1970). Measuring racial attitudes in a situational context. *Psychological Reports, 27,* 971–980.

Sergent, M. T., Woods, P. A., & Sedlacek, W. E. (1992). University student attitudes toward Arabs: Intervention implications. *Journal of Multicultural Counseling and Development, 20,* 123–131.

Sheridan, L. P. (2006). Islamophobia Pre-and Post-September 11th, 2001. *Journal of Interpersonal Violence, 21,* 317–336.

Stodghill, R., & Bower, A. (2002, August 25). Welcome to America's most diverse city. *Time.* Retrieved December 12, 2008 from http://www.time.com

White, T. J., & Sedlacek, W. E. (1987). White student attitudes toward blacks and Hispanics: Programming implications. *Journal of Multicultural Counseling and Development, 15,* 171–183.

In the United States, One County Claims Hate Crimes Go Unreported

Los Angeles County Commission on Human Relations

In the following excerpted viewpoint, the LA County Commission on Human Relations defines hate crimes broadly and argues that any hate crime is a violation of basic human rights around the world. They reveal that hate crime statistics are grossly underreported and maintain that victims must come forward and report incidents so law enforcement can appropriately investigate incidents and hold offenders accountable for their actions. The commission also insists that government entities engage in educational and outreach programs for local communities.

As you read, consider the following questions:

1. In California, where is a hate crime legally defined?
2. Can graffiti be considered a hate crime?
3. What leads to the underreporting of hate crimes?

Preface

Since 1980, the Los Angeles County Commission on Human Relations has compiled, analyzed, and produced an annual report of hate crime in the county based on data submitted by

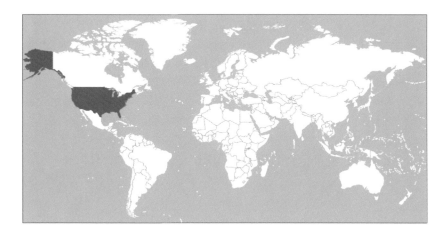

sheriff and city police agencies, educational institutions, and community-based organizations.

Using information from the report, the Commission sponsors a number of ongoing programs related to preventing and combating hate crime, including the Network Against Hate Crime, the Hate Violence Prevention Partners of LA, and the Youth Human Relations Leadership Development Initiative. L.A. County is one of the best trained jurisdictions in hate crime investigation and prosecution, and this annual report is one of the longest-standing reports in the nation documenting hate crime.

The report has been disseminated broadly to policy-makers, law enforcement agencies, educators, and community groups throughout Los Angeles County and across the nation in order to better inform efforts to prevent, detect, report, investigate, and prosecute hate crimes.

What Is a Hate Crime?

According to California state law, hate crime charges may be filed when there is evidence that bias, hatred, or prejudice based on the victim's real or perceived race/ethnicity, religion, ancestry, national origin, disability, gender, or sexual orientation is a substantial factor in the commission of the offense.

This definition is codified in the California penal code sections 422.55 to 422.95 pertaining to hate crime. Evidence of such bias, hatred, or prejudice can be direct or circumstantial. It can occur before, during, or after the commission of the offense.

Hate speech is a criminal offense when the perpetrator has threatened violence with spoken or written words against a specific person or group of persons. The threat must be immediate and unequivocal. The aggressor must also have the ability to carry out that threat. Frequently, derogatory words or epithets are directed against a member of a protected class, but no violence is threatened or there is no apparent ability to carry out the threat. Such hate incidents are important indicators of intergroup tensions. They are not, however, criminal offenses. Such language is protected by free speech rights set forth in the California and U.S. constitutions.

Graffiti is a hate crime when it is disparaging to a class of people protected by hate crime laws. This is most often indicated by the use of epithets or hate group symbols or slogans. To be a hate crime, graffiti must be directed at a specific target. For example, racial graffiti on a freeway overpass that does not address itself to a particular person is vandalism, and therefore illegal, but not considered a hate crime. Vandalism of a house of worship or of an ethnic, religious, or gay and lesbian organization may be investigated as a hate crime in the absence of evidence of other motives.

Underreporting of Hate Crimes

The National Crime Victim Survey by the U.S. Justice Department found that hate crimes occurred 22 to 40 times more than the number reported by police to the FBI[1]. This is due to victims not reporting hate crimes to police, as well as a failure of law enforcement to classify hate crimes and report them to federal authorities.

Common reasons victims don't report hate crimes to law enforcement:

- Fear of retaliation by the perpetrator(s) or friends, family, or fellow gang members of the perpetrator(s)

- Linguistic or cultural barriers

- Immigration status

- Lack of knowledge about the criminal justice system

- Fear of insensitive treatment or prior negative experience with government agencies

- Common reasons law enforcement agencies don't report hate crime:

- Hate crime reporting is a low priority

- Lack of formal hate crime policies, training, or practices

- Crimes with multiple motivations or involving gangs are frequently not reported as hate crimes

- Reluctance to admit to a problem that could result in negative publicity for the city or neighborhood

- Burden on investigating detectives in order to prove bias motivation

Hate crimes that occur in schools, jails, and juvenile detention facilities, including large-scale racial brawls, are rarely reported as hate crimes.

For all of these reasons, it is reasonable to conclude that the hate crimes included in this report likely represent only a fraction of hate crimes actually committed in 2014.

Hate Crime and Human Rights

Hate crimes are not only illegal under state and federal laws, but they violate human rights as defined by the international community[2].

In the aftermath of World War II, leaders from many nations came together to establish the Universal Declaration of Human Rights (UDHR) in 1948.

Since then, people from all over Earth have taken steps towards turning the UDHR's powerful principles into action. Since 1965, the U.S. and 176 nations have signed the International Convention on the Elimination of All Forms of Racial Discrimination (CERD), which compels signatory nations to combat racial and national origin discrimination and report to the CERD committee. Under this treaty, hate crimes are considered serious human right abuses. The CERD Committee has stressed that government action as well as inaction can violate CERD, and there is no excuse for complacency or indifference by a government toward either public or private discrimination, particularly when it involves violence.

When the U.S. and 167 other nations signed the International Covenant on Civil and Political Rights (ICCPR), they committed their nations to respect and fulfill the right to life and the security of the person "without distinction of any kind, such as race, color, sex, language, religion, political or other opinion, national or social origin, property, birth or other status." The ICCPR also requires governments to report to the Human Rights Committee on the actual measures taken to give effect to this treaty.

The U.S. Constitution states that the Constitution and Treaties are the Supreme Law of the Land. Thus, all levels of government in the U.S.—including counties, cities and school districts—and individuals have a duty to uphold these treaty obligations by addressing discrimination manifested in hate crimes.

Building on the Ten-Point Plan developed by Human Rights First (www.humanrightsfirst.org/discrimination), some of the key strategies responding to hate crime include:

- Acknowledge and/or condemn hate crimes whenever they occur. Senior leaders should send immediate, strong, public, and consistent messages that violent hate crimes—including against migrants, refugees, and asylum seekers—will be investigated thoroughly and prosecuted to the full extent of the law.

- Strengthen enforcement and prosecute offenders. Governments should ensure that those responsible for hate crimes are held accountable under the law, that the prosecution of hate crimes against any individuals regardless of their legal status in the country is a priority for the criminal justice system.

- Develop educational and transformative approaches, particular restorative justice mechanisms, for hate crime offenders. Governments need to be smarter in utilizing effective methods to heal communities and reduce recidivism.

- Monitor and report on hate crimes. Governments should maintain official systems of monitoring and public reporting to provide accurate data for informed policy decisions to combat hate crimes.

- Reach out to community groups. Governments should conduct outreach and education efforts to communities to reduce fear and assist victims, advance police-community relations, encourage improved reporting of hate crimes to the police and improve the quality of data collection by law enforcement bodies.

Footnotes

1. U.S. Department of Justice, Bureau of Justice Statistics, 2014, "Hate Crime Victimization Statistical Tables, 2004–2012"
2. We acknowledge and thank the organization Human Rights First (www. humanrightsfirst.org) for most of the substance of this section.

Periodical and Internet Sources Bibliography

The following articles have been selected to supplement the diverse views presented in this chapter.

Charlotte Alter and Josh Sanburn. "Hate Incidents Sow Fear Across US," *Time*, March 13, 2017.

Jason Cowley. "Reaching for Utopia," *New Statesman*, October 26, 2012.

Kathleen Deloughery, Ryan D. King, and Victor Asaf. "Close Cousins or Distant Relatives? The Relationship Between Terrorism and Hate Crime," *Crime & Delinquency*, September 2012.

Deborah Douglas. "Haters, Inc.," *Ebony*, September 2015.

The Economist. "Hate Crime by the Numbers," *The Economist*, December 10, 2016.

Equality Now. "Canada: Pass Legislation to Prevent the Sexual Exploitation of Women & Girls," Equality Now, http://www.equalitynow.org/action-alerts/canada-pass-legislation-prevent-sexual-exploitation-women-girls.

Thomas Fuller. "Ethnic Hatred Tears Apart a Region of Myanmar," *New York Times*, November 30, 2012.

Deepa Iyer. "Americans, Please Help End This Post 9/11 Bias," *USA Today*, August 10, 2012.

Lauren Markoe. "FBI Report Shows Surge in Anti-Muslim Attacks, Rise in Hate Crimes," *Christian Century*, December 21, 2016.

Josh Sanburn. "Why It's So Hard to Gauge Level of Hate Crimes in US," *Time*, July 2015.

Margaret Talbot. "The Story of a Hate Crime," *New Yorker*, June 22, 2015.

Kevin Whitelaw. "Rwanda Reborn," *US News & World Report*, April 23, 2007.

CHAPTER 2

The Roots of Hate Crimes

Religious Intolerance Stems from the Rise of Monotheism

Vladimir Tomek

Vladimir Tomek, who is affiliated with Ontario Consultants for Religious Tolerance, argues that a religious belief in one God and one God only gave rise to religious intolerance and hatred. He claims the Bible and the Quran both provide precedents for hate crimes and reviews major religions and cites specific passages to back up his claims.

As you read, consider the following questions:

1. How many Christian faith groups exist?
2. According to Tomek, did religious intolerance exist before a belief in only one God?
3. How effective are Bible and Quran passages in supporting Tomek's claims?

The irrationality of religious hatred, intolerance and violence

The amount of religious hatred, oppression and violence in the world is not only appalling. It is also difficult for many people to understand.

Nobody doubts that one's religion is largely the product of one's birthplace and of early teaching in their family of origin.

"Teachings of religious tolerance and intolerance in world religions," by Vladimir Tomek, September 23, 2006. Reprinted by permission.

Most people inherit their religion like their eye color. What they learn as a child is very difficult to change when they grow up. As John Hick puts it:

> "A person born in Egypt or Pakistan is very likely to be a Muslim; one born in Burma or Tibet is very likely to be a Buddhist; one born in most parts of India is very likely to be a Hindu; and one born in Britain or the U.S.A. is likely to be a Christian. If God is omnibenevolent and just ... he would not put a newborn to a disadvantage. This seems to mean only one thing: All religions give a person the same chance for salvation."

Why then should anybody become an enemy just because he or she professes a different religion? What is the root cause of intolerance?

Religious intolerance scarcely existed before the rise of monotheism. Ancient polytheistic religions worshipped numerous gods but never involved doctrinally precise professions of faith. There was no such matters as orthodoxy or heresy. The gods were mutually tolerant of one another, and the worshippers were eclectic, moving from one shrine or cult to the next without the slightest feeling of inconsistency. In Tarsus, where St. Paul grew up, as in all the towns of the ancient world outside of Judea, the gods were not jealous. They insisted that they must be offered punctiliously all honors due to them, but they did not worry about what honors were paid to other gods or men. Much later, Attila the Hun allowed members of his horde to follow whichever gods they wished, so long as they didn't interfere in each other's freedom of worship. Attila as model for religious tolerance?

In today's world, the religions of wisdom (the Eastern religions) appear to be far more tolerant than their Western counterparts, the religions of revelation. The Jews, Christians, and Muslims, who look to the Bible and the Qur'an for guidance, find hundreds of passages that can be called upon to bolster their claims that violence and hatred against enemies are not only justified but reflect the will of God. Let us have a look.

Christianity

The following comments based on the Hebrew Scriptures (Old Testament) also refer to Judaism.

There are at present over 2,400 different Christian faith groups. Most teach that their 'way' is the only way. There can be no more than one group that is completely right. But if all but one group are wrong, then perhaps all are wrong. Most religions do not accept any beliefs differing from their own. And although their own tenets or dogma proclaim that faith, hope, and love are their foundations, many of them still commit atrocities in the name of some unseen God who, they claim, demands it.

One point of conflict comes from how the Bible itself is viewed. Many progressive and mainline Christians, believe that numerous biblical passages are not factually accurate, are ethically doubtful, conflict with other statements, or allow a diversity of interpretations. Many conservative Christians maintain that Scripture is God's Word: Their authors were directly inspired by God. Thus, their writings are inerrant. It remains a puzzle why the creator allowed the Bible's authors to produce statements that are so ambiguous that thousands of individual belief systems have resulted.

The Bible contains many commandments inciting religious intolerance, such as: Exodus 23:32, Exodus 34:14, Deuteronomy 5:7, Deuteronomy 6:15; Deuteronomy 7:25, Deuteronomy 13:6-9, Deuteronomy 17:2-7, 2 Chronicles 15:13, Jeremiah 10:2, Matthew 12:30, Luke 11:23, and Romans 16:17.

In order to become more tolerant, we would have to ignore some biblical passages. As a minimum, these would include:

- The commandments inciting people to kill, such as Deuteronomy 13:6-9; Deuteronomy 17:2-7; 2 Chronicles 15:13.

- The commandment telling us to avoid unbelievers (Romans 16:17).

It would also be helpful if Christians were skeptical of:

- Passages in the Bible derived from other religions, such as those in nearby Middle-Eastern Pagan cultures, Egyptian religion, Mithraism, etc.

- Events, beliefs and policies which were typical for the society and conditions prevailing in biblical times but are no longer applicable today.

It must be recognized that we must be prepared to abandon dogmas and teachings unworthy of the present age, however important part of the creed they seem to be. It can be done. In North America, we painfully abandoned human slavery as profoundly immoral in spite of the many biblical passages allowing, regulating and condoning it. Most denominations have abandoned the instruction to be fruitful and multiply by allowing couples to regulate their family size. Canada and the U.S. have extended freedom to religious minorities. We no longer execute homosexuals and Witches. Most denominations allow women to enter almost any profession, including the ministry.

Early Christians were guided by the compassionate teaching of Christ. However, the situation degenerated during the 4th century CE when, following Constantine's conversion, Christianity was first accepted as a legitimate religion, and later became identified with the state.

Perhaps one of the most intolerant of the early Christian leaders was St. Ambrose (c.339-397), one of the four original Doctors of the Western Church. In his debate with Ambrose in the Roman senate, the pagan Symachus argued eloquently for religious tolerance. In reply, Ambrose maintained that there was only one "correct religion." All the others should be viciously and quickly stamped out.

Another important person was Hypatia (circa 370–415 CE). She was the head of the Neoplatonic School of Alexandria. A physicist, mathematician, astronomer, philosopher, and spokesperson for the Alexandrian library, she was known for her un-Christian idea of refusing to marry and to "be fruitful and multiply." On the suspicion that she had set the pagan prefect of Alexandria against the Christians, fanatical Christians, inspired by the archbishop of Alexandria Cyril, dragged her from her chariot. In front of her friends and students, they cut away the flesh from her bones, burned her remains, and destroyed her work.

During the Renaissance, tens of thousands of people, mostly women, were arrested on charges of heresy, and were burned at the stake (in Catholic countries) or hanged (in Protestant countries).

In more modern times, the Bible was used to provide the European settlers with an ideology that justified exterminating Native Americans. Particularly remembered is the famous speech by Cotton Maher in 1689 given to the armed forces, when he accused Natives of murdering Christians. Native Americans were almost wiped out by the Europeans who understood Indians as Amalekites and Canaanites, Indian land as equivalent to Canaan, and themselves as God's chosen people.

In another part of the world, Palestinian Christians are shocked when the Bible is used to justify the Israeli occupation of their homeland.

Unitarianism

Unitarianism (called Unitarian Universalism in the U.S.) was once considered a very liberal Christian denomination. It has since become a multi-faith group, whose members may personally identify themselves as Christian, Buddhist, Native American, Pagan, Humanist, Atheist, Agnostic, etc.

Unitarianism is necessarily bound to oppose any form of dogmatism and finality. It tends to reject those religious belief systems that claim to have one final prophet with whom divine revelations are 'sealed.' Unitarians believe that people must be free "to work out their own salvation" and to formulate their own beliefs in the light of their own experience. The latter may be gained by studying with open mind the Bible (which is not considered infallible), some other holy text(s), or simply by serious thought, prayer and dialogue with others. The three fundamental principles of Unitarianism are: Freedom, Reason, and Tolerance.

As stated by John Hostler:

> "Unitarians have gone beyond the toleration of other denominations, and have embraced the ideal of religious freedom. They insist that even in Unitarianism shared beliefs are not essential, and every member of a religious community ought to be completely free to hold and develop his own convictions."

Islam

Prior to the early 20th century, religious minorities in predominately Islamic countries were treated reasonably well. Non-Muslims were required to pay a special tax. However, they were not subject to the intense persecution that religious minorities experienced in predominately Christian countries.

Khalid Baig writes in his essay on religious tolerance:

> "Not only that the Muslim history is so remarkably free of the inquisitions, persecutions, witch hunts, and holocausts that tarnish history of other civilizations, it protected its minorities from persecution by others as well. It protected Jews from Christians and Eastern Christians from Roman Catholics. In Spain under the Umayyads and in Baghdad under the Abbasid *Khalifahs*, Christians and Jews enjoyed a freedom of religion that they did not allow each other or anyone else."

> "This exemplary tolerance is built into Islamic teachings. The entire message of Islam is that this life is a test and we have the option of choosing the path to hell or to heaven. Messengers were sent to inform about the choices and to warn about the consequences. They were not sent to forcibly put the people on the right path. The job of the Muslims is the same. They must deliver the message of Islam to the humanity as they have received it. They are neither to change it to make it attractive, nor to coerce others to accept it. In addition, the results in the hereafter will depend upon faith. For all good acts are meaningless in the absence of the proper faith. And faith is an affair of the heart. It simply cannot be imposed."

Muslims believe that the Islamic faith is grounded in beliefs which are absolute and final. The Qur'an is regarded as the literal word of God, a divine utterance that is uncreated and co-eternal with Him. The Qur'an contains, in addition to purely Islamic materials, a number of passages that are paralleled by those in the Hebrew and Christian Scriptures (Old and New Testaments). However, Islamic teaching maintains that the Divine message as preserved in the Bible is corrupt and distorted. The belief that the Qur'an is the word of God renders the discussions of Biblical sources of the Qur'an irrelevant for Muslims.

Belief in the Qur'an is not based on reason, logic or philosophy. It is to be accepted without question or condition. The name Islam is derived from the Arabic word "salam," which can be translated as "submission." Muhammad-Baqer Majlisi, one of the greatest doctors of Shi's theology, wrote: "A man who thinks is sending signals to Satan." Theological dialogue is often considered the prerogative of theologians who clarify issues for believers.

The Qur'an, the holy book of Islam, contains verses requiring Muslims to express tolerance towards other religions, particularly towards Jews and Christians. All three are the "people of the Book" who share a reverence for Abraham. But there are other verses which close to door to any possible understanding between Muslims and followers of other religions:

- The main verses supporting the acceptance of the other monotheistic religions are: II.59, II.257, III.77, and CIX. Less supportive are verses XXIII.56 and LXXIII.10.

- Note that verse XI.257 "There shall be no compulsion in religion" is followed by a verse indicating that the unbelievers will be brought into the shadows and will remain in the fire forever.

- The main verses clearly advocating intolerance and containing injunction to fight unbelievers are: II.187, III.27, III.114, IV.91, IV.144, V.37, V.56, VIII.65, IX.5, IX.29, IX.125, XXV.54, and XLVII.4. These verses are very unambiguously stated.

Those verses in the Qur'an that indicate a positive attitude towards other monotheistic religions are often quoted by Muslims to show that Islam is a friendly religion intent on peaceful cooperation with other religions. Ahmad Mahmud Soliman states that:

> "Islam orders its adherents not only to tolerate the opinions and creeds of others, but also have a firm belief in the orthodox principles of all heavenly religions. A Muslim who disbelieves the other apostles (such as Jesus or Moses) is not a true Muslim. Islam forbids the ill treatment of the followers of other religions and regards it as sinful to do them harm."

Unfortunately, it is the other verses that are more frequently quoted by radical fundamentalist mullahs. These verses imply that there can be neither relationship nor friendship, not even peaceful co-existence of Muslims with non-Muslims. These include verses such as:

- IX.29 "Fight those who do not believe;"
- IX.5 "Slay the pagans wherever you fight them," and
- II.187 "Slay them wherever you catch them."

Islamic theologians use the principle of abrogation to determine the correct Qur'an teaching. Abrogation, which is based on Sura II.100, is not expressly stated in the Qur'an. Its criteria is if there is a discrepancy between two Qur'anic texts, the more recent text cancels out the earlier one. By extension, the Qur'an is claimed to abrogate all previously revealed Scriptures. Similarly, Muhammad's prophethood supersedes the missions of all previous prophets.

Unfortunately, there are serious problems with the application of this principle:

- How can there be a discrepancy in an inerrant text dictated by an Archangel?
- The doctrine of abrogation conflicts with the Qur'anic affirmation that Allah's word, i.e., the Qur'an, is unchangeable (Suras X.64, XVIII.26, VI.115).

- The exact dates or even the precise chronological order of the Suras cannot be determined. This makes it difficult or impossible to determine which parts of the revelation were meant to be abrogating and which not abrogated.

Not surprisingly, radical ulama (theologians) tend to annul passages that are friendly to non-Muslims. There can be no question of tolerance toward other religions. The abrogating verses, the verses that remain valid, are then the verses commanding the faithful to fight and kill the unbelievers.

In the Qur'an, Islam is stated to be the complete religion which Allah has chosen for humanity. It follows that any religious innovations must steer clear of anything that might be interpreted as apostasy. This makes religious change extremely difficult.

In the U.N. Declaration of Human Rights, the clause which affirms a person's right to freely change his or her religion if he or she so wishes, runs directly counter both the Islamic law on apostasy and to the practice of execution of persons who leave Islam—a response still enforced by some of the more conservative Muslim states.

Islam is almost entirely fundamentalist. "Under Islam it is not religion that is part of life, but life a part of religion." (Habib Boulares) Among the best-known Islamic fundamentalist movements are the Muslim Brotherhood and the Islamic Party (Jama'at-I Islami), and there are many extremist offshoots. The original goal of the Muslim Brotherhood, was the reform of Islamic society by eliminating Western influence. Its current goal is the creation of theocratic Islamic states. The original purpose of the Islamic Party was to train a cadre of future leaders capable of rebuilding the Muslim society. Its main interest seems to lie still in education, although science is considered intrinsically evil. The Hezb-Allah (the Party of Allah) was founded by Ayatollah Mahmoud Ghaffari in Qom in 1973. In 1987, it boasted a membership of more than a million in the Islamic Republic of Iran alone.

Extremist Islamic fundamentalism cannot conceive of either coexistence or political compromise. A world based on religious and political diversity is repugnant to them. Their goal seems to be a world ruled by a theocratic dictatorship based on the Qur'an and Islam. Their teaching justifies or even requires violence, terrorism, and war against enemies, in service to Allah.

However, there are also moderate voices within Islam. Some live in the west in countries where Muslims are in a small minority. Some commentators predict that it will be from western countries that a reform movement will arise to make major changes to Islam.

If the world is to avoid the spiral of violence that threatens us, we must have sufficient doubt and skepticism to challenge historical interpretations of some passages in the Bible, Qur'an, and other holy texts. We need to go beyond the distorted images of God which wrongly associate divine and human power with superior violence and defeat of enemies, which form part of ancient understanding of these texts.

The Bahá'í Faith

The Bahá'í faith advocates cultural and religious tolerance as one of its main teachings. Bahá'u'lláh instructed his followers to associate with all the peoples of the world: The Bahá'ís should "consort with the followers of all religions in a spirit of friendliness and fellowship". 'Abdu'l-Bahá advocated "infinite kindness and forbearance" when speaking with those of a different religion. He claimed that "fanaticism and unreasoning religious zeal repel others", and that "shunning others because of their religious beliefs, regarding them as ritually unclean, and treating them with discourtesy, are to be condemned." Even when 'Abdu'l-Bahá strongly disagreed with the religious beliefs of others he avoided directly criticizing them, except when these beliefs engendered social attitudes of which he disapproved, such as racial hatred and religious intolerance. These teachings contrasted with the 19th-century Iranian Shi'a practice to discriminate against minority religious groups (such as Zoroastrians, Jews, and Christians) and regard them as ritually unclean. The Bahá'í tolerant approach was very likely a factor in the conversion of members of those groups.

According to the Bahá'í, reducing differences among religions is needed in order to build a common religious approach. This requires change and flexibility on the part of all religions, along with the elimination of all fundamentalist, absolutist, orthodox, and conservative attitudes with their à priori stances. The fundamentalist approach, based on insight from immutable revelation, dogma, and inerrant received wisdom must be replaced by a more openness. There is nothing to be afraid of if we follow what we believe in. "Our Father will not hold us responsible for the rejection of dogmas which we are unable either to believe in or comprehend, for He is infinitely just to His children." ('Abdu'l-Bahá.)

According to Bahá'u'lláh "every man and woman is responsible for what he or she believes and should not blindly imitate anyone". The only danger is that when we believe that ours is the only faith that contains truth, violence and suffering will surely be the result. Is it not reason enough to try to avoid contentious claims?

In the Bahá'í view, of all the causes of religious intolerance the most prevalent is "ignorance and lack of understanding of the most basic elements of the various religious beliefs." Thus, it would appear that education is one of the paths to the elimination of religious intolerance.

The Bahá'í are convinced that the world is moving inexorably toward unity and tolerance of diversity—even diversity of religion and belief. They believe that the principle of religious tolerance is gaining acceptance.

The Bahá'í are probably the most advanced of all the major religions as far as religious tolerance is concerned. However, even with them not everything is perfect: Bahá'í scholars are forbidden to change, delete or otherwise reinterpret Bahá'u'lláh's writings and 'Abdu'l-Bahá's interpretations and explanations of them. This inability to change is causing the Bahá'í faith to fall behind the positions of other liberal religions concerning homosexuality.

Sikhism

Sikhism has successfully combined elements from Bhakti Hinduism, Advaita, and Sufism, with emphasis upon tolerance and coexistence between Muslim and Hindus. It was based on mutual respect of the two communities. Whether Sikhism is seen as an attempt to reconcile Hinduism and Islam by creating a syncretism, or in some other light, its existence gave hope that religious reconciliation does not have to be an empty word.

Unfortunately, the hope has practically disappeared. Misused religion became a distant second to politics. Between 1981 and 1994, thousands of young men and perhaps a few hundred women were initiated into secret fraternities of various rival radical Sikh organizations. These included the Babbar Khalsa, the Khalistan Commando Force, the Khalistan Liberation Force, the Bhindranwale Tiger Force of Khalistan, and extremist factions of the All-India Sikh Student Federation. Their enemies were secular political leaders, heads of police units, Hindu journalists, and community leaders. Over the time the distinction between valid and inappropriate targets became blurred and virtually anyone could become a victim of the militants' wrath.

- In 1984-JUN, Sikh terrorists seized the Sikh holy shrine, the Golden Temple in Amritsar. Many people were killed, including a number of innocent worshippers, when Indian security forces re-took the temple.

- In 1984-DEC, Mrs. Gandhi was assassinated by her Sikh bodyguards as revenge for this act of profanity. On the following day more than two thousand Sikhs were massacred in Delhi and elsewhere as a reprisal.

- In 1991, over three thousand people were killed during disturbances in the Punjab.

- In 1991 the Sikh extremists attacked the Indian ambassador to Romania. The Romanian government helped to capture the

Sikhs. Later that year militant Sikhs kidnapped a Romanian diplomat in Delhi in retaliation. And so on.

Buddhism, Hinduism, Jainism, and Taoism

These religions have a tradition of religious tolerance and of respecting religious diversity. However, they are all able to embrace positions of violence as well as non-violence, of religious tolerance as well as of intolerance.

Buddhism does not support war or any type of violence, and any expression of religious intolerance has to be seen as an exception. In Hinduism, the first virtue to be practiced is ahimsa, the doctrine of non-violence, which is also part of the Buddhist and Jain teachings. Ahimsa was interpreted by Gandhi as 'non-violence in a universal sense' and elevated to the foremost human quality.

Hinduism can still be considered non-violence and religious tolerance friendly, but there are some disturbing signs.

- The Bengali terrorists fighting the British colonial rule used the Bhagavad Gita as a sacred script in support of their doctrines. One of their manifestos contained the following words: "Take up arms and protect religion. When one is face to face [with the enemy], they should be slaughtered without hesitation. Not the slightest blame attaches to the slayer. … Lay down your life but first take a life …."

- Mahatma Gandhi was assassinated by a Hindu fundamentalist, Nathuram Godse.

- The doctrine of Hindutva asserts that Hinduism, as the 'indigenous' faith of India, must be dominant, and that all 'foreign' religions must be subject to the will of the majority.

- Hindu fundamentalism is manifested in the family of Hindu nationalist organizations known as Sangh Parivar. In 1992, Sangh Parivar activists stormed and destroyed the 16th century mosque in Ayodha, setting off riots between Muslims and Hindus throughout India in which thousands were killed.

- For a time, a certain form of fundamentalism has exerted considerable impact on Indian mainstream politics. The Bharatiya Janata Party (BJP) was formed in 1980 as the political expression of Hindutva.

- According to Jainism, each person has the freedom of choice to act his life out according to his own wishes; the freedom of choice applies also to his or her religion. This is the doctrine of anekantvada (many-sidedness) which posits that truth is intensely personal.

- The doctrine of ahimsa gives Jainism (as well as Hinduism and Buddhism) a strong pacifist streak.

- Daoism (a.k.a. Taoism) is unique in the importance it assigns to pacifism, and in its opposition to ambition, worldly authority, and political power. There is a well-documented cooperation of Daoism and Confucianism.

References

Henry Bamford Parkes, "Gods and Men," Routledge and Keegan Paul, (1960).

Bart D. Ehrman, "Lost Christianities," Oxford University Press, (2003).

Andrew Norman Wilson, "Paul," Pimlico, (1998).

Jack Nelson-Pallmeyer, "Is Religion Killing Us?" Trinity Press International, (2003).

Sumner W Davis, "Heretics," 1stBooks, (2001).

Susan Niditch, "War in the Hebrew Bible," Oxford University Press, (1993).

John Hostler, "Unitarianism," The Hibbert Trust, (1981).

Khalid Baig, "On religious tolerance," at: http://www.youngmuslims. ca/

Taheri Amir, "Holy Terror. Inside the World of Islamic Terrorism." Adler & Adler, (1987).

Mahmud Soliman Ahmad, "Scientific Trends in the Qur'an," Ta-Ha, (1995).

Helmut Gatje, "The Qur'an and its Exegesis," Oneworld, (1996).

Faruq Sherif, "A Guide to the Contents of the Qur'an," Garnet Publishing, (1999).

Johannes J.G Jansen, "The Dual Nature of Islamic Fundamentalism," Hurst, (1997).

The Ku Klux Klan's Reign of Hate-based Terror in the United States

The Klanwatch Project

In the following excerpted viewpoint, writers from the Southern Poverty Law Center's Klanwatch Project argue that the roots of the racist Ku Klux Klan remain a mystery to many people today. They claim slavery, the Civil War, and Reconstruction led to the formation of this secret, night-riding group. After a resurgence in power following World War I, the Klan remains active, although weakened. The Klanwatch Project was established in 1981 to help stifle the Klan and other acts of racist violence by monitoring activity, litigating cases, and educating the public.

As you read, consider the following questions:

1. When and where did the Ku Klux Klan form?
2. Was it founded as a racist terrorist group?
3. What do members of the Klan wear?

The Terror is Born: The Founding of the Ku Klux Klan

The bare facts about the birth of the Ku Klux Klan and its revival half a century later are baffling to most people today. Little more than a year after it was founded, the secret society thundered across the war-torn South, sabotaging Reconstruction governments and

"Ku Klux Klan—A History of Racism and Violence," compiled by the staff of the Klanwatch Project of the Southern Poverty Law Center, The Southern Poverty Law Center. Reprinted by permission.

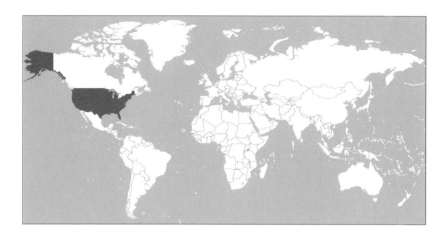

imposing a reign of terror and violence that lasted three or four years. And then as rapidly as it had spread, the Klan faded into the history books. After World War I, a new version of the Klan sputtered to life and within a few years brought many parts of the nation under its paralyzing grip of racism and bloodshed. Then, having grown to be a major force for the second time, the Klan again receded into the background. This time it never quite disappeared, but it never again commanded such widespread support.

Today, it seems incredible that an organization so violent, so opposed to the American principles of justice and equality, could twice in the nation's history have held such power. How did the Ku Klux Klan—one of the nation's first terrorist groups—so instantly seize the South in the aftermath of the Civil War? Why did it so quickly vanish? How could it have risen so rapidly to power in the 1920s and then so rapidly have lost that power? And why is this ghost of the Civil War still haunting America today with hatred, violence and sometimes death for its enemies and its own members?

Frontier Justice

The answers do not lie on the surface of American history. They are deeper than the events of the turbulent 1960s, the parades and cross burnings and lynchings of the 1920s, beyond even the Reconstruction era and the Civil War. The story begins, really, on the frontier, where successive generations of Americans learned hard lessons about survival. Those lessons produced some of the qualities of life for which the nation is most admired—fierce individualism, enterprising inventiveness, and the freedom to be whatever a person wants and to go wherever a new road leads.

But the frontier spirit included other traits as well, and one was a stubborn insistence on the prerogative of "frontier justice"—an instant, private, very personal and often violent method of settling differences without involving lawyers or courts. As the frontier was tamed and churches, schools and courthouses replaced log trading posts, settlers substituted law and order for the older brand of private justice. But there were always those who did not accept the change. The quest for personal justice or revenge became a key motivation for many who later rode with the Ku Klux Klan, especially among those who were poor and uneducated.

Night Patrols

A more obvious explanation of the South's widespread acceptance of the Klan is found in the institution of slavery. Freedom for slaves represented for many white Southerners a bitter defeat—a defeat not only of their armies in the field but of their economic and social way of life. It was an age-old nightmare come true, for early in Southern life whites in general and plantation owners in particular had begun to view the large number of slaves living among them as a potential threat to their property and their lives.

A series of bloody slave revolts in Virginia and other parts of the South resulted in the widespread practice of authorized night patrols composed of white men specially deputized for that purpose. White Southerners looked upon these night patrols as a civic duty, something akin to serving on a jury or in the militia. The mounted patrols, or regulators, as they were called, prowled Southern roads, enforcing the curfew for slaves, looking for runaways, and guarding rural areas against the threat of black uprisings. They were authorized by law to give a specific number of lashes to any violators they caught. The memory of these legal

The Unusual Origins of the Klan

The origin of the Ku Klux Klan was a carefully guarded secret for years, although there were many theories to explain its beginnings. One popular notion held that the Ku Klux Klan was originally a secret order of Chinese opium smugglers. Another claimed it was begun by Confederate prisoners during the war. The most ridiculous theory attributed the name to some ancient Jewish document referring to the Hebrews enslaved by the Egyptian pharaohs.

In fact, the beginning of the Klan involved nothing so sinister, subversive or ancient as the theories supposed. It was the boredom of small-town life that led six young Confederate veterans to gather around a fireplace one December evening in 1865 and form a social club. The place was Pulaski, Tenn., near the Alabama border. When they reassembled a week later, the six young men were full of ideas for their new society. it would be secret, to heighten the amusement of the thing, and the titles for the various offices were to have names as preposterous-sounding as possible, partly for the fun of it and partly to avoid any military or political implications. Thus the head of the group was called the Grand Cyclops. His assistant was the Grand Magi. There was to be a Grand Turk to greet all candidates for admission, a Grand Scribe to act as secretary, night hawks for messengers and a Lictor to be the guard. The members, when the six young men found some to join, would be called Ghouls. But what to name the society itself?

The founders were determined to come up with something unusual and mysterious. Being well-educated, they turned to the Greek language. After tossing around a number of ideas, Richard R. Reed suggested the word "kuklos," from which the English words "circle" and "cycle" are derived. Another member, Capt. John B. Kennedy, had an ear for alliteration and added the word "clan." After tinkering with the sound for a while they settled on Ku Klux Klan. The selection of the name, chance though it was, had a great deal to do with the Klan's early success. Something about the sound aroused curiosity and gave the fledgling club an immediate air of mystery, as did the initials K.K.K., which were soon to take on such terrifying significance.

Soon after the founders named the Klan, they decided to do a bit of showing off, and so disguised themselves in sheets and galloped their horses through the quiet streets of tiny Pulaski. Their ride created such a stir that the men decided to adopt the sheets as the official regalia of the Ku Klux Klan, and they added to the effect by donning grotesque masks and tall pointed hats. They also performed elaborate initiation ceremonies for new members. Similar to the hazing popular in college fraternities, the ceremony consisted of blindfolding the candidate, subjecting him to a series of silly oaths and rough handling, and finally bringing him before a "royal altar" where he was to be invested with a "royal crown." the altar turned out to be a mirror and the crown two large donkey's ears. ridiculous though it sounds today, that was the high point of the earliest activities of the Ku Klux Klan.

Had that been all there was to the Ku Klux Klan, it probably would have disappeared as quietly as it was born. But at some point in early 1866, the club added new members from nearby towns and began to have a chilling effect on local blacks. The intimidating night rides were soon the centerpiece of the hooded order: bands of white-sheeted ghouls paid late night visits to black homes, admonishing the terrified occupants to behave themselves and threatening more visits if they didn't. It didn't take long for the threats to be converted into violence against blacks who insisted on exercising their new rights and freedom. Before its six founders realized what had happened, the Ku Klux Klan had become something they may not have originally intended—something deadly serious.

night riders and their whips was still fresh in the minds of both defeated Southerners and liberated blacks when the first Klansmen took to those same roads in 1866.

Aftermath of War

An even more immediate impetus for the Ku Klux Klan was the Civil War itself and the reconstruction that followed. When robed Klansmen were at their peak of power, alarmed Northerners justifiably saw in the Klan an attempt of unrepentant Confederates to win through terrorism what they had been unable to win on the battlefield. Such a simple view did not totally explain the Klan's sway over the South, but there is little doubt that many a Confederate veteran exchanged his rebel gray for the hoods and sheets of the Invisible Empire.

Finally, and most importantly, there were the conditions Southerners were faced with immediately after the war. Their cities, plantations and farms were ruined; they were impoverished and often hungry; there was an occupation army in their midst; and reconstruction governments threatened to usurp the traditional white ruling authority. In the first few months after the fighting ended, white Southerners had to contend with the losses of life, property and, in their eyes, honor. The time was ripe for the Ku Klux Klan to ride.

Mischief Turns Malicious

Robert E. Lee's surrender was not fully nine months past when six young ex-confederates met in a law office in December 1865 to form a secret club that they called the Ku Klux Klan. From that beginning in the little town of Pulaski, Tennessee, their club began to grow. Historians disagree on the intention of the six founders, but it is known that word quickly spread about a new organization whose members met in secret and rode with their faces hidden, who practiced elaborate rituals and initiation ceremonies.

Much of the Klan's early reputation may have been based on almost frivolous mischief and tomfoolery. At first, a favorite Klan tactic had been for a white-sheeted Klansman wearing a ghoulish mask to ride up to a black family's home at night and demand water. When the well bucket was offered, the Klansman would gulp it down and demand more, having actually poured the water through a rubber tube that flowed into a leather bottle concealed beneath his robe. After draining several buckets, the rider would exclaim that he had not had a drink since he died on the battlefield at Shiloh. He then galloped into the night, leaving the impression that ghosts of Confederate dead were riding the countryside.

The presence of armed white men roving the countryside at night reminded many blacks of the pre-war slave patrols. The fact that Klansmen rode with their faces covered intensified blacks' suspicion and fear. In time, the mischief turned to violence. Whippings were used first, but within months there were bloody clashes between Klansmen and blacks, Northerners who had come South, or Southern unionists. From the start, however, there was also a sinister side to the Klan.

Ethnicity Is the Primary Motivation for Hate Crimes

Meagan Meuchel Wilson

In the following excerpted viewpoint, US Department of Justice statistician Meaghan Meuchel Wilson argues that—based on the number of reported hate crimes at the federal level—there was no statistically significant change between 2004 and 2012, even with the 2009 amending of the Hate Crime Statistics Act. However, given this, she also claims that the majority of hate crimes reported were based on the victim's ethnicity and that these crimes, along with those motivated by bias against religion and gender, increased.

As you read, consider the following questions:

1. In 2012, what percentage of hate crimes in the United States were perceived to have an ethnic bias?
2. The 2009 Hate Crimes Statistics Act defined incidents of hate crime against which targeted group to be unlawful?
3. Which organizations collect hate crime data for the US government?

In 2012, an estimated 293,800 nonfatal violent and property hate crime victimizations occurred against persons age 12 or older residing in U.S. households. The apparent increase from 2011 to 2012 in the rate of overall violent hate crime was not statistically significant (figure 1).

"Hate Crime Victimization, 2004–2012—Statistical Tables," by Meagan Meuchel Wilson, Bureau of Justice Statistics, February 2014. Reprinted by permission.

Figure 1

Violent hate crime victimizations reported and not reported to police, 2004-2012

Rate per 1,000 persons age 12 or older
Note: Detail may not sum to total due to rounding and missing data. Hate crime includes

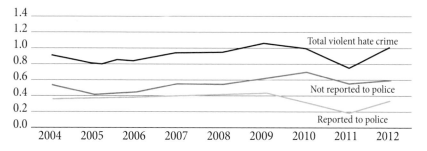

incidents confirmed by police as bias-motivated and incidents perceived by victims to be bias-motivated because the offender used hate language or left behind hate symbols. Estimates were based on 2-year rolling averages centered on the most recent year. See appendix table 1 for estimates and standard errors.

SOURCE: Bureau of Justice Statistics, National Crime Victimization Survey. 2003-2012.

The findings from this report came primarily from the Bureau of Justice Statistics' (BJS) National Crime Victimization Survey (NCVS), which has been collecting data on crimes motivated by hate since 2003. The NCVS and the FBI's Uniform Crime Reports (UCR) Hate Crime Statistics Program, which are the principal sources of annual information on hate crime in the United States, use the definition of hate crime provided in the Hate Crime Statistics Act (28 U.S.C. § 534). The act defines hate crimes as "crimes that manifest evidence of prejudice based on race, gender or gender identity, religion, disability, sexual orientation, or ethnicity." The NCVS measures crimes perceived by victims to be motivated by an offender's bias against them for belonging to or being associated with a group largely identified by these characteristics.

Hate crime victimization refers to a single victim or household that experienced a criminal incident believed by the victim to be motivated by hate. For violent crimes (rape or sexual assault, robbery, aggravated assault, and simple assault) and for personal larceny, the count of hate crime victimizations is the number of individuals who experienced a violent hate crime. For crimes against households (burglary, motor vehicle theft, and other theft), each household affected by a hate crime is counted as a single victimization.

This report presents NCVS data on the characteristics of hate crimes and hate crime victims from 2003 to 2012. Trend estimates are based on 2-year rolling averages centered on the most recent year. This method generally improves the reliability and stability of estimate comparisons over time. For ease of discussion, the report refers to all 2-year estimates by the most recent year. For example, estimates reported for 2012 represent the average estimates for 2011 and 2012. The report also compares NCVS and UCR overall trends in hate crime victimization.

Number and rate of hate crimes

- In 2012, hate crimes accounted for 1.2% of all victimizations and 4.2% of violent victimizations.

- No statistically significant change was observed in either the number of total hate crimes or violent hate crimes that occurred from 2004 to 2012.

- After a decline from 2004 to 2005, the property hate crime victimization rate remained stable from 2005 to 2012.

Hate crime motivation

- Approximately 58% of hate crime victims reported more than one type of motivation in 2012.

- In 2012, victims perceived that the offender was motivated by bias against the victim's ethnicity in 51% of hate crimes.

This was a statistically significant increase from 30% of hate crimes motivated by ethnicity bias in 2011 and 22% in 2004.

- The percentage of hate crimes motivated by religious bias was nearly three times higher in 2012 (28%) than in 2004 (10%), but did not have a statistically significant change from 2011 to 2012.

- In 2009, Congress passed new legislation amending the Hate Crime Statistics Act to include hate crimes with evidence of bias against a particular gender or gender identity. BJS has been collecting information on hate crimes motivated by gender bias since 2003. The percentage of hate crimes motivated by gender bias was more than two times higher in 2011 (25%) and 2012 (26%) than in 2004 (12%).

Differences between hate and nonhate crimes

- Each year from 2004 to 2012, violent crimes accounted for a higher percentage of hate crimes than nonhate crimes.

- The percentage of hate crimes involving violence increased from 78% in 2004 to 90% in both 2011 and 2012. However, no statistically significant difference was observed in the percentage of hate crimes involving serious violence or simple assault in these years.

- In 2012, serious violent crime accounted for a higher percentage of all hate crime victimizations (27%) than nonhate crime victimizations (8%).

- In 2012, no statistically significant difference was observed between the percentage of violent hate crimes (30%) and violent nonhate crimes (31%) that involved serious violence.

Weapons and injuries

- In 2012, the offender had a weapon in at least 24% of violent hate crime victimizations.

- No statistically significant difference was reported between the percentage of violent hate (24%) and violent nonhate (20%) crime victimizations in which the offender was known to have a weapon in 2012.

- The percentage of violent hate and violent nonhate crime victimizations in which the offender was known to have a weapon remained stable from 2011 to 2012.

- In 2012, the victim sustained an injury in about 20% of violent hate crime victimizations.

- No statistically significant difference was observed in 2012 between the percentage of violent hate (20%) and violent nonhate (24%) crime victimizations in which the victim sustained an injury.

- The percentage of violent hate and violent nonhate crime victimizations in which the victim sustained an injury remained stable from 2011 to 2012.

Hate crimes reported to the police

- An estimated 60% of total and violent hate crime victimizations were not reported to police in 2012. This was a slight decline from 2011, when about three-quarters of total (74%) and violent (73%) hate crime victimizations were not reported to police.

- Overall, the percentage of hate crime victimizations that resulted in the victim signing a complaint or the police making an arrest did not have a statistically significant change from 2011 to 2012.

Violent hate crime victim and offender characteristics

- From 2011 to 2012, rates of violent hate crime victimization did not have a statistically significant change for either males or females.

- In 2011, violent hate crime victimization rates were similar among white non-Hispanics, black non-Hispanics, and Hispanics. However, in 2012, Hispanics experienced a higher rate of violent hate crime victimization (2.0 victimizations per 1,000 residents) than whites (0.8 per 1,000) and a slightly higher rate than blacks (1.1 per 1,000).

- The rate of violent hate crime victimization against Hispanics more than tripled from 0.6 per 1,000 persons age 12 or older in 2011 to 2.0 per 1,000 in 2012.

- The rate of violent hate crime victimization increased for persons ages 18 to 24 (from 0.6 per 1,000 in 2011 to 2.0 in 2012) and for persons ages 50 to 64 (from 0.4 to 0.9 per 1,000), while the rate declined for persons ages 25 to 34 (from 1.6 to 0.7 per 1,000). Violent hate crime victimization rates for persons in all other age groups did not have a statistically significant change from 2011 to 2012.

- Persons residing in households with an income greater than $50,000 per year experienced a higher rate of violent hate crime victimization in 2012 (1.0 per 1,000) than in 2011 (0.4 per 1,000).

- In both 2011 and 2012, persons living in households with an income of $24,999 or less per year experienced the highest rate of violent hate crime victimization (2.1 per 1,000), compared to persons residing in all other households (1.0 or less per 1,0001).

- From 2011 to 2012, no statistically significant change was observed in the percentage of violent hate crimes committed by either a single offender or by multiple offenders.

- In 2012, the percentage of violent hate crimes committed by a single offender (64%) was higher than the percentage committed by two or more offenders (34%).

- Each year from 2004 to 2012, victims reported that males committed the majority of violent hate crimes.

- The percentage of violent hate crime victims who perceived the offender to be white decreased from 58% in 2011 to 34% in 2012. However, the percentage of white offenders was similar in 2004 and 2012.

- The percentage of offenders ages 18 to 29 declined from 29% in 2011 to 13% in 2012. In 2012, persons age 30 and over made up the largest percentage of hate crime offenders (41%).

- In 2012, the percentage of violent hate crimes committed by someone known to the victim was slightly higher (53%) than the percentage committed by a stranger (40%).

Hate crimes recorded by the NCVS and UCR

- The FBI's UCR collects data on hate crimes known to the police. It includes offenses excluded from the NCVS, such as murder or non-negligent manslaughter, intimidation, arson, vandalism, and crimes against institutions (e.g., churches, synagogues, and businesses). The NCVS collects data on hate crimes both reported and not reported to police and allows the victim to define whether a hate crime occurred.

- Hate crime victimizations recorded by the UCR declined steadily from 2008 to 2012. However, no statistically significant change was observed in NCVS hate crime victimizations reported to police from 2008 to 2012.

- UCR hate crime victimizations were lower in 2012 than in 2004. No statistically significant difference was observed between the number of NCVS hate crime victimizations reported to police in 2004 (127,390) and 2012 (98,460).

- Based on data from the NCVS, persons age 12 or older experienced an annual average of 269,140 hate crime victimizations from 2004 to 2012, of which 105,890 were reported to police **(figure 2)**.

- According to the NCVS, an annual average of 14,380 hate crime victimizations were confirmed by police investigators

Figure 2

NCVS and UCR hate crime victimizations, 2004-2012

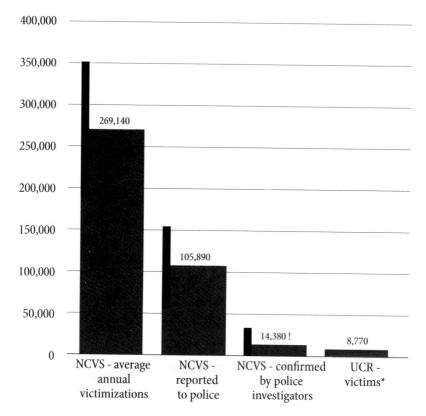

Annual average victimizations

Note: Hate crime includes incidents confirmed by police as bias-motivated and incidents perceived by victims to be bias-motivated because the offender used hate language or left behind hate symbols. Estimates were based on 10-year rolling averages due to small sample sizes. Numbers rounded to the nearest ten. Error bars on NCVS estimates are based on 95% confidence levels. The standard error for average annual victimizations is 40,701; reported to police is 24,180; and confirmed by police investigators is 8,345.

*Includes murder/non negligent manslaughter, forcible rape, aggravated assault, simple assault, intimidation, other crimes against persons, robbery, burglary,larceny-theft, motor vehicle theft, arson, destruction/vandalism, other crimes against property, and crimes against society.

! Interpret with caution; estimate based on 10 or fewer cases, or the coefficient of variation is greater than 50%.

Gwen Araujo Murdered Ten Years Ago Today

Today marks the tenth anniversary of the brutal murder of transgender teenager Gwen Araujo in Newark, California.

Only 17 years old at the time of her death, today Gwen would be a 27-year-old young woman had her life not been brutally taken by four men who discovered she was born male.

The story of Gwen's life has been celebrated and kept alive by her mother, Sylvia Guerrero. Sylvia supported Gwen when she transitioned as a teenager, and in an act of love and respect, had her child's name legally changed to Gwen after the murder.

In 2006, Lifetime aired a TV Movie about Gwen's life and the tragic manner in which it ended. *A Girl Like Me: The Gwen Araujo Story* stars J.D. Pardo (currently starring in *Revolution* on NBC) and Mercedes Ruehl. The film received the GLAAD Media Award for Outstanding TV Movie, and can be seen via Amazon Instant Video.

Gwen's murder brought much-needed attention to the horrific nature and frequency of violent hate crimes against transgender people. In 2006, then-Governor Arnold Schwarzenegger signed into law the "Gwen Araujo Justice for Victims Act," which states that the use of societal bias, including so-called "panic strategies," to influence the proceedings of a criminal trial is not permitted.

Unfortunately transgender people, especially transgender women of color, continue to be targeted for vicious and brutal attacks.

Every year, communities around the United States hold the annual Transgender Day of Remembrance in November. This event remembers and draws attention to the dozens of transgender people murdered every year simply for being themselves.

"Gwen Araujo Murdered Ten Years Ago Today," by Nick Adams, GLAAD, October 3, 2012

from 2004 to 2012. This estimate was not statistically different from the FBI's UCR annual average number of hate crime victims (8,770) during the same period.

In South Africa, the United States Provides a Model for Hate Crime Laws

Kamban Naidoo

In the following viewpoint, law professor Kamban Naidoo, who teaches at the University of South Africa in Pretoria, details how, despite the widespread definition and legislation of hate crime laws in much of the Western world, South Africa has yet to establish stringent laws against hate crime. Naidoo claims that the United States stands as a model of hate crime law and cites two specific historical periods—post-Civil War and post-World War II until the civil rights movement—that led to recognition of a specific category of crimes known as hate crimes.

As you read, consider the following questions:

1. Which amendment to the US Constitution granted African-Americans citizenship?
2. What did the Civil Rights Act of 1866 guarantee?
3. Which US law recognized criminal conduct motivated by prejudice or basis based on a victim's race, color, religion, or national origin?

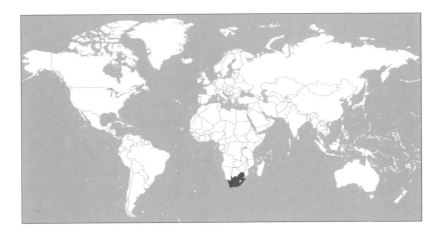

Abstract

Hate crimes were first recognised as a specific category of criminal conduct in the United States of America. Evidence of such recognition is supported by a number of state level and federal hate-crime laws that were enacted in the United States between the early 1980s and 1990s. There is a tendency in some American literature, however, to trace the recognition of hate crime as a specific category of criminal conduct to two specific historical time periods. The first historical period that is usually considered, is the nineteenth-century post-American Civil War period when federal civil-rights statutes were passed by the American Congress to protect vulnerable groups of people who were victimised because of their race and prior status as slaves. The second time period that is considered is the mid-twentieth century, post-Second World War era up to the period of the Civil-Rights Movement. Irrespective of the origins of hate crime as a category of criminal conduct, their recognition has spawned a new category of crime and criminal laws in the United States of America and internationally. Contemporary hate-crime laws recognise a wide spectrum of prejudices and biases. Despite the international trend, particularly in democratic Western nations towards the recognition of hate crimes and the enactment of hate-crime laws, the Republic of South Africa has yet to enact a hate-crime law.

Introduction

The non-recognition of hate crime as a specific category of criminal conduct in South African law has prompted recent calls for the enactment of hate-crime legislation.[1] A hate crime may be described as criminal conduct which is motivated by the perpetrator's prejudice or bias, commonly referred to as "hate", towards the victim's race, ethnicity, gender, sexual orientation, religion, disability and several other victim characteristics.[2]

A hate crime therefore consists of conduct which complies with the definition of a crime and which is motivated by the perpetrator's bias or prejudice against the victim.[3] In most jurisdictions that recognise hate crime as a specific category of criminal conduct, laws have been enacted which create specific hate crimes[4] and which allow sentencing officers to impose harsher sentences on convicted hate-crime perpetrators; these are referred to as aggravated or enhanced penalties.[5]

Several academic scholars agree that the United States of America has been at the forefront of the enactment of hate-crime legislation for more than two decades.[6] While the recognition of hate crime as a category of criminal conduct undoubtedly has its roots in the United States of America, there is no consensus as to the date when criminal conduct motivated by specific prejudices or biases was first accorded such recognition in American history.[7] This article attempts to trace the origins of both hate crime as a specific category of criminal conduct as well as hate-crime laws.

Post-American Civil-War origins of hate-crime laws

Several writers trace the origins of hate-crime laws to the post-Civil War period in the United States of America when the American Congress passed numerous federal civil-rights laws.[8] Petrosino[9] opines that the "antecedents" of present hate-crime laws can be traced to the post-Civil War or "Reconstruction" period which culminated in a number of legal reforms and constitutional amendments. A similar view is expressed by Levin[10] who sees the "seeds" of present American hate-crime laws in post-Civil War laws which protected groups of people on the basis of their status, and in particular on the basis of their race.

The foundations of the American civil-rights model were laid during the post-Civil-War period. The American Congress ratified several amendments to the Constitution: the Thirteenth Amendment in 1865 abolished slavery, the Fourteenth Amendment in 1868 granted citizenship to all persons born or nationalised in the United States of America and the Fifteenth Amendment in 1870 extended voting rights to citizens who were previously denied this right because of their race, colour or status as slaves.[11] All the aforementioned Constitutional amendments included provisions for Congress to pass legislation to enforce the amendments at state level thereby removing the autonomy of states to deprive minorities of their rights.[12] A number of federal statutes were subsequently passed during this period which supplemented and enforced the constitutional amendments and which protected newly-freed slaves, especially in the Southern states where they were "at best second-class citizens and at worst subject to harassment, intimidation and murder".[13]

The reluctance of state-level local authorities to prosecute crimes committed by Whites against Blacks[14] led to the American Congress passing the Civil Rights Act of 1866 which established citizenship for all those born in the United States of America and the Enforcement Act of 1870, which guaranteed the rights of due process of law and equal protection of the law guaranteed by the Fourteenth Amendment, and the right to vote established by the Fifteenth Amendment.[15]

According to the Civil Rights Act of 1866[16:]

all persons born in the United States and not subject to any foreign power, excluding Indians not taxed, are hereby declared to be citizens of the United States; and such citizens, of every race and colour, without regard to any previous condition of slavery or involuntary servitude, except as punishment for crime whereof the party shall have been duly convicted, shall have the same right in every State and Territory in the United States, to make and enforce contracts, to sue, be parties, and give evidence, to inherit, purchase, lease, sell, hold, and convey real and personal property, and to full and equal benefit of all laws and proceedings for the security of persons and property, as is enjoyed by white citizens, and shall be subject to like punishment, pains, and penalties, and to none other, any law, statute, ordinance, regulation, or custom, to the contrary notwithstanding.

In the above statute citizenship and class or group-based protection were extended to all races (except for certain categories of Native Americans or "Indians"), to former slaves and generally to people of colour.

Levin describes the period of Reconstruction as follows:[17]

New, sweeping Constitutional and statutory reforms cut off the traditional legal and political methods Whites relied upon to deprive Blacks of their rights ... although their initial success was fleeting, these new, egalitarian post-war reforms laid the foundation for changes that extended into the latter half of the next century, including the emergence of hate-crime laws.

The American Congress also passed the Civil Rights Act of 1871 which permitted the federal government to prosecute people who conspired to deprive others of their civil rights or to prosecute government agents who deprived persons of their rights. According to the Civil Rights Act of 1871,[18]

[w]hoever, under colour of any law, statute, ordinance, regulation, or custom, subjects any person in any State, Territory, Commonwealth, Possession or District to the deprivation of any rights, privileges, or immunities secured or protected by the Constitution or laws of the United States, or to different punishments, pains, or penalties, on account of such person being an alien, or by reason of his colour, or race, than are prescribed for the punishment of citizens, shall be fined under this title or imprisoned for not more than a year, or both; and if bodily injury results from the acts committed in violation of this section, or if such acts include the use, attempted use,

or threatened use of a dangerous weapon, explosives, or fire, shall be fined under this title or imprisoned not more than ten years, or both; and if death results from the acts committed in violation of this section or if such acts include kidnapping or an attempt to kidnap, aggravated sexual abuse or an attempt to commit aggravated sexual abuse, or an attempt to kill, they shall be fined under this title or imprisoned for any term of year or for life, or both, or may be sentenced to death.

Jacobs and Potter[19] opine that the purpose of the Civil Rights Act of 1871 was to guarantee fair law enforcement irrespective of the race of the victim. Levin[20] is of the view that these civil-rights laws consisted of "a protected group ... a covered activity ... and a prohibition on some type of detrimental conduct".[21] The 1871 Act further extended protection to classes or groups of people, in this instance to "aliens" and to persons on the basis of race and colour. According to Levin[22] these laws "represented a newfound validation of federal authority in the area of criminal law and supremacy of national power over that of the states to protect minorities from the harms of race-based violence and discrimination".[23]

The American Congress also enacted the Ku Klux Klan Act of 1871 which expanded the federal government's power to intervene where states failed to protect the constitutional rights of its citizens. The Ku Klux Klan Act of 1871 permitted federal authorities to intervene in an enumerated list of activities where there was a conspiracy to violate civil rights, for example threatening government officials, intimidating witnesses and jurors at a federal trial, and interfering with a citizen's right to equal protection under the law and a citizen's voting rights. These were among the conspiracies that were practised by the Ku Klux Klan against Blacks.[24]

The American Congress further passed the Civil Rights Act of 1875 which provided for equal treatment of all races in public accommodation, facilities, transport and places of entertainment.[25]

Jacobs and Potter[26] regard the various federal civil-rights laws referred to above as "federal-criminal civil-rights statutes" since they were the only option available to the federal government to ensure that crimes committed against former slaves at local and state level would be investigated and prosecuted. If state and local authorities had investigated and prosecuted crimes against former slaves there would have been no need for the enactment of these statutes. During the Reconstruction period one also finds some judicial recognition accorded to racial bias motivation albeit in a dissenting judgement only. According to Lawrence,[27] Justice Bradley "anticipated the modern development of bias-crime law, reading the Thirteenth Amendment as a font of federal authority for all crimes committed with racial animus" in the case of *United States v Cruikshank*.[28]

In the case of Cruikshank Justice Bradley opined that in order to federalise a common-law crime[29]:

> There must be a design to injure a person, or deprive him of his equal right of the protection of the laws, by reason of his race, colour, or previous condition of servitude ... otherwise it is a case exclusively within the jurisdiction of the state and its courts.

According to Levin hate crimes belong to a "subset" of old civil-rights and antidiscrimination laws.[30] He therefore does not regard the present recognition of hate crime as a specific category of criminal conduct as a novel phenomenon. Jacobs and Potter,[31] however, argue that while federal civil-rights statutes dealt with issues of race and discrimination, as some hate-crime laws do, this is the only similarity that these laws have with the present American régime of hate-crime legislation. They further opine that the civil-rights statutes of the Reconstruction era were not aimed at hate crimes as the concept is presently understood, but were intended to deal with interference with a person's civil rights. Moreover, the federal civil-rights laws of the nineteenth century did not enhance penalties and recriminalise conduct already criminalised in law.[32]

The twentieth-century origins of hate-crime laws

There is some suggestion that the recognition of hate crime as a specific category of criminal conduct and the origin of hate-crime laws may be traced to the post-Second World War period when bigotry based on race, ethnicity and gender were increasingly condemned by American society.[33]

During this period the state of Connecticut was one of the first American states to pass a statute which addressed the problem of "racially-motivated assaults". The Connecticut General Statute of 1949 "criminalised the ridiculing of an individual based on race, colour or creed".[34] Petrosino[35] suggests that the origin of modern hate-crime laws in the United States of America could also be linked to the 1954 United States Supreme Court decision in *Brown v Board of Education of Topeka*[36] which overturned the "separate but equal" doctrine in American public schools.[37]

Some scholarly research traces the origins of hate-crime laws in the United States of America to the Civil-Rights Movement[38] of the 1960s, the women's rights and the gay and lesbians' rights movement of the 1970s as well as the subsequent disabilities and victims' rights movement.[39] Jacobs and Potter regard the Civil Rights Movement of the 1960s as significant since it resulted in the development of "identity politics" which they link to the modern hate-crime movement as follows[40]:

> [I]dentity politics refers to a politics whereby individuals relate to one another as members of competing groups based upon characteristics like race, gender, religion and sexual orientation. According to the logic of identity politics, it is strategically advantageous to be recognised as disadvantaged and victimised. The greater a group's victimisation, the stronger its moral claim on the larger society. the current hate-crime movement is generated not by an epidemic of unprecedented bigotry but by heightened sensitivity to prejudice and, more important, by our society's emphasis on identity politics.

According to Hall[41], after the Civil-Rights Movement there followed a shift in thinking in relation to the treatment of certain minority groups. The advantages to be gained in recognising a group's prior mistreatment and victimisation included official recognition in a number of social contexts such as employment benefits, university admissions, the awarding of public contracts and the creation of voting districts[42]. In terms of the logic of identity politics, "a group can assert a moral claim to special entitlements and affirmative action"[43]. In a similar vein, Jenness and Grattet write that[44]:

> The anti-hate crime movement emerged through a fusion of the strategies and goals of several identifiable precursor movements that laid the foundation for a new movement to question and make publicly debateable, issues of rights and harm as they relate to a variety of constituencies.

These diverse social movements, in asserting their respective demands, stimulated public discussions about violence based on prejudice and bigotry and began demanding legal changes, especially in criminal law, to address the problem[45]. According to Jenness,[46] these movements politicised and emphasised violence against minority groups because of their minority status: the Civil-Rights Movement politicised violence against racial minorities (such as police brutality against Blacks), the women's-rights movement politicised violence against women (such as rape and domestic violence), the gay and lesbian-rights movement politicised violence against homosexuals (such as "gay bashing") and the disabilities movement politicised violence against people with disabilities (such as "mercy killings"). The predominant issue that these diverse civil-rights movements had in common was the perpetration of violence against specific minority groups. A later social movement to have a significant influence on the development of hate-crime laws was the victims' rights movement which emphasised that the victims of crime, especially violent crimes, have the right to special assistance such as counselling services, increased participation in the criminal-justice process, civil remedies and other special protections[47]. The modern anti-hate crime movement thus arose out of these diverse social movements representing the interests of different groups of victims who have been aptly referred to as "strange bedfellows"[48].

A significant American law which was passed as a result of the Civil-Rights Movement and which may be considered as a precursor of modern hate-crime laws was the Civil Rights Act of 1968[49]. Although this Act was not aimed at hate crimes per se, it is considered as a "catalyst for modern hate-crime legislation"[50]. The Civil Rights Act of 1968 prohibits interference with a person's federally-protected rights in cases of violence or threats of violence because of a person's race, colour, religion or national origin. The federally-protected rights include, inter alia, the rights to vote, to public education, to participation in jury service, to interstate travel and access to public places and services. According to Wang[51], the Civil Rights Act of 1968 requires the defendant to have acted with a bias motive since it uses the words because of the victim's protected status and that prior to the creation of a purely federal hate-crime law, the American federal government resorted to the use of this Act to prosecute hate crimes. The Civil Rights Act of 1968 places the onus on the prosecution to prove that the defendant was motivated by bias and attacked the victim who was engaged in a federally-protected activity[52].

Jacobs and Potter[53] write that the Civil Rights Act of 1968 was intended to provide a remedy for the violence that resulted from opposition to civil-rights marches, to voter registration and voting issues, to the admission of Black students to formerly all-white schools and universities and to efforts to abolish the laws that enforced segregation. However, the complicated nature of the Civil Rights Act of 1968[54] and the high burden of proof required to secure convictions led to the emergence of state-level hate-crime laws in the United States of America with less onerous evidentiary requirements[55].

As the Civil-Rights Movement gained momentum, civil-society organisations such as the Anti-Defamation League[56] and the Southern Poverty Law Centre[57] began compiling statistical reports to establish the number and frequency of crimes motivated by prejudice, bias and bigotry[58]. In 1981 the Anti-Defamation League, concerned by the rise in crimes motivated by racial and ethnic bias and prejudice in the United States of America, particularly anti-Semitic crimes, and the fact that media exposure, education and law enforcement were ineffective, drafted a model hate-crime statute which recognised racial, religious and ethnic biases[59]. It should be noted at this point that gender and sexual orientation biases were only subsequently added to an amended model hate-crime statute[60]. The model statute was intended to influence state legislatures and the Federal government to enact hate-crime laws. The Anti-Defamation League's model hate-crime statute had the desired effect since a number of state legislatures in the United States of America subsequently enacted laws based on the model statute[61]. Shortly after the drafting of the Anti-Defamation League's model hate-crime statute in 1981, the states of Oregon and Washington passed similar laws[62]. According to Gerstenfeld[63], while many states used the Anti-Defamation League's model as a prototype, they often made changes, while other states drafted their own original statutes. Gerstenfeld[64] writes that this is the reason for the diversity of hate-crimes laws in the United States of America today.

Perhaps the most significant federal law of the modern hate-crimes era to be passed in the United States of America was the Hate Crime Statistics Act of 1990, which has been briefly referred to in the introduction to this article. What is particularly significant about this statute is that the term "hate crime" was first coined by three members of the House who were sponsoring the Bill when being debated in the American House of Representatives[65]. Jacobs and Potter66 acknowledge representatives John Conyers, Barbara Kennelly and Mario Biaggi, who used the term "hate crime" in 1985 to refer to crimes motivated by racial, religious and ethnic prejudice.

From 1985, the term "hate crime" entered media and social discourse in the United States of America and appeared in eleven newspaper articles nationwide[67]. Ehrlich[68] opines that his term "ethnoviolence" which had hitherto been commonly used to refer to criminal conduct motivated by bias and prejudice was replaced by the term "hate crime" since it was a term that appealed to issues of crime, law and social control which were considered as legitimate issues by the media popularising such issues. The Hate Crimes Statistics Act simply obliged the United States Department of Justice to collect statistics of hate-crime incidents across the United States of America[69].

Conclusion

The origins of hate-crime laws and the recognition of hate crime as a specific category of criminal conduct are shrouded in some uncertainty. The existing research suggests that shortly after the American Civil War laws were enacted which provided for status-based protection. However, the federal civil-rights laws which were passed during this period of American history were intended to protect vulnerable groups on the basis of race or previous conditions of servitude but did not provide for enhanced or aggravated penalties. The ostensible precursor of modern hate-crime laws can be traced to the period of the Civil Rights Movement which culminated in the enactment of the Civil Rights Act of 1968. This was one of the earliest American laws to specifically recognise criminal conduct motivated by prejudice or bias towards a victim based on the victim's race, colour, religion or national origin. However, the Civil Rights Act of 1968 also did not allow for the imposition of enhanced or aggravated penalties.

It is submitted that the criminalisation of conduct motivated by prejudice and bias (or "hate") and the imposition of enhanced or aggravated penalties for crimes that are motivated by racial, ethnic, gender or sexual orientation bias reflect the abhorrence with which such crimes are viewed by modern, democratic societies.

The imposition of enhanced or aggravated penalties therefore reflects modern society's denunciation of criminal conduct that is motivated by such biases[70]. Since hate crimes that are motivated by the race, ethnicity or sexual orientation of the victim conflict with society's established, acceptable values, they may be punished more severely.

Since the enactment of the Hate Crimes Statistics Act in 1990 a number of federal hate-crime laws have been passed in the United States of America. Contemporary hate-crime laws recognise a wide spectrum of victim characteristics that includes race, ethnicity, religion, disability, gender and sexual orientation. These hate-crime laws include the Hate Crimes Sentencing Enhancement Act of 1994 and the Matthew Shepherd and James Byrd Junior Hate Crimes Prevention Act of 2009. To date, over forty-five American states and the District of Columbia have enacted hate-crime statutes based on the Anti-Defamation League's model statute[71]. The American trend to enact hate-crime laws has had some international impact, particularly in Western democratic countries. In 1998 the United Kingdom passed the Crime and Disorder Act which is the British equivalent of a hate-crime law and in 2003 France passed its first hate-crime law, which is commonly referred to as la loi Lellouche[72].

In South Africa, civil-society organisations have made several submissions to the Department of Justice which have recommended the enactment of hate-crime legislation[73]. It is lamentable that these calls have not been heeded given postapartheid South Africa's status as a constitutional state and its commitment to equality[74]. While hate-crime laws will not eradicate crimes motivated by bias and prejudice, the imposition of the criminal sanction and an aggravated penalty to such conduct may be considered as the ultimate "symbolic message"[75] that a government has at its disposal to try and change prejudiced attitudes and the manifestations thereof.

Bibliography
Books, journals and websites

Bleich, Erik (2008) "Responding to racist violence in Europe and the United States" in Goodey, Jo & Aromaa, Kauko (eds) *Hate Crime: Papers from the 2006 and 2007 Stockholm Criminology Symposium* (Helsinki): 9-15

"Civil rights: An overview" (accessed 30 Jul 2015): available at http://www.cornell.edu/wex/civilrights

Duncan, Breen & Nel, Juan N (2011) "South Africa—A home for all? The need for hate-crime legislation" *SA Crime Quarterly* 38: 33-42

Ehrlich, Howard J (2009) *Hate Crime and Ethnoviolence: The History, Current Affairs and Future of Discrimination in America* (Boulder, Colo)

Freeman, Steven M (1992-1993) "Hate-crime laws: Punishment which fits the crime" *Annual Survey of American Law* 4: 581-585

Gerstenfeld, Phyllis B (2013) *Hate Crimes: Causes, Controls and Controversies* 3 ed (Thousand Oaks, Calif)

Grattet, Ryken & Jenness, Valerie (2004) "The birth and maturation of hate-crime policy in the United States" in Gerstenfeld, Phyllis B & Grant, Diana R (eds) *Crimes of Hate: Selected Readings* (Thousand Oaks, Calif): 23-44

Hall, Nathan (2013) *Hate Crime* 2 ed (Abingdon)

Harris, Bronwyn (accessed 11 Nov 2015) "Arranging prejudice: Exploring hate crime in post-apartheid South Africa" available at http://www.csvr.org.za/docs/racism/arrangingprejudic.pdf)

Howard, Alan B (ed) (accessed 30 Jul 2015) "Website of the Southern Poverty Law Center" available at http://www.splcenter.org/who-we-are/splc-history

Henderson, Elizabeth K (2010) "Offended sensibilities: Three reasons why the Hate Crimes Prevention Act of 2009 is a well-intended misstep" *Chapman LR* 2: 163-195

Iganski, Paul (2002) "Hate crimes hurt more, but should they be punished more severely?" in Iganski, Paul (ed) *The Hate Debate: Should Hate Be Punished as a Crime* (London): 132144

Jacobs, James B & Potter, Kimberley (1998) *Hate Crimes, Criminal Law and Identity Politics* (New York, NY)

Jacobs, James B (1992-1993) "Implementing hate crime-legislation, symbolism and crime control" *Annual Survey of American Law* 4: 541-553

Jenness, Valerie (2002) "Contours of hate crime politics and law in the United States" in Iganski, Paul (ed) *The Hate Debate: Should Hate be Punished as a Crime?* (London): 15-34

Lawrence, Frederick M (1999) *Punishing Hate: Bias Crimes under American Law* (Cambridge, Mass)

Levin, Brian (1999) "Hate crimes: Worse by definition" *J of Contemporary Criminal Justice* 15(1): 6-21

Levin, Brian (2002) "From slavery to hate crime-laws: The emergence of race and status-based protection in American criminal law" *J of Social Issues* 58(2): 227-245

Levin, Brian (2009) "The long arc of justice: Race, violence and the emergence of hate crime-law" in Perry, Barbara *et al Hate Crimes* vol 1 (Westport, Conn): 1-22

Meese, Ed (1997) "Big Brother on the beat: The expanding federalization of crime" *Texas Rev of Law and Politics* 1: 1-23

Mollema, Nina & Van der Bijl, Charnelle (2014) "Hate crimes: The ultimate anathematic crimes" *Obiter* 35(3): 672-679

Naidoo, Kamban & Karels, Michelle (2012) "Hate crimes against black lesbian South Africans: Where race, sexual orientation and gender collide (Part 2)" *Obiter* 33(3): 600-624

Petrosino, Carolyn (1999) "Connecting the past to the future: Hate crime in America" *J of Contemporary Criminal Justice* 15(1): 22-47

Shimamoto, Eric (2003-2004) "Rethinking hate crime in the age of terror" *University of Missouri-Kansas City LR* 72: 829-843

"The Civil Rights Act of 1871" (accessed 30 Jul 2015) available at http://www.arch.ksu.edu/jwkplan/law/civil%20rights%20 acts%20of%201866,%2018

Walker, Samuel (1994) *Hate Speech: The History of an American Controversy* (Lincoln, Neb)

Wang, Lu-in (2000) "Recognising opportunistic bias crimes" *Boston University LR* 80: 1399-1435

"Website of the Anti-Defamation League" (accessed 1 Aug 2015) available at http://www.adl.org/PressRele/HatCr_51/5635_51.htm

"Website of the Hate Crimes Working Group" (accessed 1 Jul 2015) available at http://www.hcwg.org.za/HCWG

Legislation

France

Loi No 2003-88 du 3 février 2003

South Africa

The Constitution of the Republic of South Africa, 1996

The Promotion of Equality and Prevention of Unfair Discrimination
Act 4 of 2000
United Kingdom
The Crime and Disorder Act, 1998 (c 37)
United States of America
The Civil Rights Act of 1866 14 Stat 27-30
The Enforcement Act of 1870 16 Stat 140
The Civil Rights Act of 1871 17 Stat 13
The Ku Klux Klan Act of 1871 17 Stat 13
The Civil Rights Act of 1875 18 Stat 335-337
Connecticut General Statute of 1949 c 14
Civil Rights Act of 1968 82 Stat 73
Hate Crime Statistics Act of 1990 28 USC § 534
The Hate Crimes Sentencing Enhancement Act of 1994 28 USC 994
The Matthew Shepard and James Byrd Junior Hate Crimes
Prevention Act of 2009 18 USC § 249

Case law

United States of America

Brown v Board of Education, Topeka 347 US 483 (1954)
United States v Cruikshank 25 Fed Cases 707 (1874)

Footnotes

1 In this regard see Duncan & Nel 2011: 33; Naidoo & Karels 2012: 624; and Mollema &
Van der Bijl 2014: 679. See, also, Harris (accessed 11 Nov 2015). Most of the present South
African public and academic debate surrounding the non-recognition of hate crime in
South African law and the need for hate-crime laws concern sexual orientation in light of
the rapes and murders of Black lesbian women. However, calls for hate-crime legislation
also concern race and ethnicity following the large-scale outbreaks of xenophobic
violence against black African foreigners in 2008 and 2015. It should be noted that despite
the non-recognition of hate crime as a specific category of criminal conduct in South
African criminal law, hate-speech provisions exist in South Africa. Sections 10 and 12
of the Promotion of Equality and Prevention of Unfair Discrimination Act 4 of 2000
(hereinafter referred to as the Promotion of Equality Act) contain specific prohibitions
on hate speech. These provisions are applicable to the publication and dissemination of
words and information that could incite harm or promote hatred towards a specific group
of people. This statute provides a civil remedy for hate speech in the form of damages. The
conduct that is prohibited by the Promotion of Equality Act does not, however, address
physically violent and coercive criminal conduct that is motivated by prejudice or bias.
The Promotion of Equality Act therefore does not afford protection to most victims of
hate crimes in South Africa.
2 Since hate crimes are crimes that are motivated by bias or prejudice, there is a tendency
in some American literature to refer to hate crimes as "bias crimes". However the term
"hate crime" will be used in this article.

3 In the context of hate-crime laws, the crime is referred to as the "underlying" crime, or the "base" or the "predicate" crime. The motivation is regarded as a "bias motivation". See, further, Lawrence 1999: 9.

4 If, eg, a crime of assault is motivated by prejudice or bias towards the race of the victim, the bias motivation would render the crime a racially-motivated assault and consequently as a hate crime.

5 An aggravated or enhanced penalty is more severe than the penalty imposed on the same crime when it is not motivated by bias or prejudice towards the victim's race, ethnicity, sexual orientation, gender etc. See, in this regard, s 7 of the American statute, the Matthew Shepard and James Byrd Junior Hate Crimes Prevention Act of 2009 as well as s 28 of the British statute, the Crime and Disorder Act of 1998, which allow for the imposition of enhanced or aggravated penalties on convicted hate-crime perpetrators.

6 Levin 1999: 6; Gerstenfeld 2013: 31-32; Hall 2013: 18.

7 The earliest example of a contemporary federal hate-crime law in the USA is the Hate Crime Statistics Act of 1990. This latter Act may be considered as the first modern federal hate-crime law in the USA. However, as will become clear below, several American states had enacted their own hate-crime laws during the early 1980s.

8 Levin 2002: 227; Hall 2013: 20; Gerstenfeld 2013: 12-13.

9 1999: 15.

10 2002: 228.

11 See Hall 2013: 21; Levin 2002: 231.

12 See Hall 2013: 21. Section 5 of the Fourteenth Amendment gave Congress the power to pass any laws necessary to enforce the amendment. See "Civil rights: An overview" (accessed 30 Jul 2015).

13 Lawrence 1999: 122. Lawrence cites the examples of the 1866 New Orleans and Memphis riots in which many Blacks were killed, as well as the increasing attacks on freed slaves by the Ku Klux Klan and smaller organised hate groups such as the Knights of White Carmelia and the White Brotherhood (see, in general, Lawrence 1999: 199-200).

14 Jacobs & Potter 1998: 36.

15 See Lawrence 1999: 22.

16 Quoted from "The Civil Rights Act of 1866" (accessed 30 Jul 2015).

17 See Levin 2002: 231.

18 Quoted from "The Civil Rights Act of 1871" (accessed 30 Jul 2015).

19 1998: 37.

20 2009: 4.

21 The "protected group(s)" refer specifically to persons of colour, freed slaves and aliens. The "covered activities" included the exercise of property rights, contractual rights, litigation and due process of law (in terms of the Civil Rights Act of 1866). The "prohibited conduct" included a general prohibition against violent behaviour, with or without the use of weapons, kidnapping and sexual abuse (in terms of the Civil Rights Act of 1871).

22 2002: 231.

23 According to Hall 2013: 47, during this period of American history, a debate raged between states and the federal government over control of criminal law enforcement. According to Meese 1997: 6, the drafters of the American Constitution had intended crime and law enforcement to fall largely within the jurisdiction of states.

24 According to Lawrence 1999: 122-123, during the congressional debates on the Bill, the intention was to provide federal authorities with the right to intervene in a number of common-law crimes such as murder, arson and robbery. However, the Bill was amended and federal prosecution was then limited to the specified activities. Thus, rather than a

broad, hate-crime law, the Ku Klux Klan Act of 1870 confined federal criminal jurisdiction only to cases of "rights-interference crimes".

25 According to the Civil Rights Act of 1875 " ll persons within the jurisdiction of the United States shall be entitled to full and equal enjoyment of the accommodations, advantages, facilities and privileges of inns, public conveyances on land or water, theatres, and other places of public amusement, subject only to the conditions and limitations established by law, and applicable alike to citizens of every race and colour, regardless of any previous condition of servitude". It is submitted that the Civil Rights Act of 1875 is an early example of an anti-discrimination law.

26 1998: 36.

27 1999: 127.

28 United States v Cruikshank 25 Fed Cases 707 (1874).

29 United States v Cruikshank 25 Fed Cases 707 (1874) at 712.

30 2009: 3.

31 1998: 36.

32 Ibid.

33 This is an alternative view that is expressed by Jacobs & Potter 1998: 5. According to Henderson 2010: 164, in order to avert a genocide like the Holocaust, a number of international treaties were negotiated in the post-Second World War period which were designed to eradicate incitement to racial discrimination (which, in turn, led to the 1965 International Convention on the Elimination of All Forms of Racial Discrimination) and to prohibit advocacy of national, religious and racial hatred (which resulted in the 1966 International Covenant on Civil and Political Rights). It would be trite to add that in the immediate aftermath of the Second World War there was increased international awareness of bigotry, prejudice and racism and the devastating consequences thereof.

34 See Lawrence 1999: 20. In this regard, refer to ss 53 to 57 of the Connecticut General Statute of 1949.

35 1999: 15.

36 347 US 483 (1954).

37 While it is conceded that the case of Brown v Board of Education of Topeka marked a new, more liberal direction in the jurisprudence of the American Supreme Court, Petrosino does not provide any convincing proof that the origins of hate-crime laws can be traced to this period.

38 According to Shimamoto 2003-2004: 831, the Civil-Rights Movement refers to a period commencing in the early 1960s that was marked by violent protests and demonstrations, sit-ins and marches against racist practices and segregation in the USA.

39 See, eg, Jacobs 1992-1993: 542; Jacobs & Potter 1998: 5; Grattet & Jenness 2004: 23-24; and Jenness 2002: 19-22.

40 1998: 5-6.

41 2013: 23.

42 See Jacobs & Potter 1998: 66.

43 Ibid.

44 2004: 26.

45 See Grattet & Jenness 2004: 25-26.

46 2002: 20.

47 See Grattet & Jenness 2004: 26.

48 See Jenness 2002: 21.

49 See Jacobs & Potter 1998: 38.

50 See Hall 2013: 24.

51 2000: 1401.

52 According to Wang 2000: 1402-1403, the Civil Rights Act of 1968 was a difficult statute to invoke in hate crimes since it required proof of bias motivation in order to fulfil the culpability requirements and that a victim's "enumerated right" had been interfered with or that the victim was engaged in a "federally-protected activity".

53 1998: 38.

54 Ibid.

55 See Hall 2013: 114.

56 The Anti-Defamation League of B'nai B'rith (or the ADL) is a civil-rights organisation that was formed in 1913, initially with a focus on anti-Semitism, but subsequently countering all forms of discrimination and infringements of civil rights. See Walker 1994: 18.

57 The Southern Poverty Law Center (SPLC) was formed in the southern American state of Alabama by a group of civil-rights lawyers in 1971. Its mission was to test civil-rights laws and to seek justice for the poor and disenfranchised. See Howard (accessed 30 Jul 2015).

58 See Grattet & Jenness 2004: 26.

59 Freeman 1992-1993: 582.

60 See Grattet & Jenness 2004: 27.

61 See Freeman 1992-1993: 583.

62 See Gerstenfeld 2013: 31.

63 Ibid.

64 Ibid.

65 See Hall 2013: 25.

66 1998: 4.

67 Ibid.

68 2009: 18.

69 See Lawrence 1999: 22.

70 In this regard, see Iganski 2002: 138.

71 See the "Website of the Anti-Defamation League" (accessed 1 Aug 2015).

72 Which may be translated as "the Lellouche law". The full title of the "Lellouche law" is Loi No 2003-88 du 3 février 2003. See Bleich 2008: 12.

73 Refer to the "Website of the Hate Crimes Working Group" (accessed 1 Jul 2015). As has been stated in the introduction to this article, these calls for the enactment of hate-crime laws should be considered in light of the crimes that have been perpetrated against black lesbian women and the large-scale outbreaks of xenophobic violence against black African foreigners in South Africa.

74 The Constitution of the Republic of South Africa, 1996, which includes a justiciable Bill of Rights, is regarded as supreme law. The right to equality is enshrined in s 9 of the Constitution. It is submitted that the victims of crimes motivated by race, ethnicity and sexual orientation cannot fully enjoy their rights as equal citizens in a democratic South Africa until the enactment of hate-crime laws.

75 See Hall 2013: 124.

Bias at the Heart of the Pulse Shooting

UPDATED...

Officials announced at a 10:15 AM EDT news conference that the number of dead in this morning's Orlando mass shooting has risen to 50.

DEVELOPING...

A shooting rampage at an Orlando, Florida nightclub early Sunday left "approximately 20" people dead, including the gunman, and 42 injured, authorities said.

At a 7 AM EDT news conference, Police Chief John Mina said the shooting began at 2:02 a.m., when three police officers engaged in a gun battle with a suspect outside Orlando Pulse, an LGBTQ club just south of downtown. A hostage situation then took place inside, and a SWAT team was called in, Mina said. Police received updates from patrons trapped in the club, and decided to storm the club at about 5 a.m.

"We exchanged gunfire with the suspect, and he was dead at the scene", Mina said.

Javer Antonetti, 53, told the Orlando Sentinel that he was near the back of the dance club when he heard gunfire. "There were so many (shots), at least 40," he said. "I saw two guys and it was constant, like 'pow, pow, pow.'"

Mina said 42 people were transferred to local hospitals, and one officer was wounded. He estimated the death toll at 20, and said at least 30 people were rescued.

"Tonight our community witnessed a horrific crime... that will have a lasting effect on our community," Orlando Mayor Buddy Dyer said.

"Do we consider this an act of terrorism? Absolutely, we are investigating this from all parties' perspective as an act of terrorism," said Danny Banks, special agent in charge of the Florida Department of Law Enforcement Danny Banks.

Accurate Reporting Is a Key to Understanding Hate Crimes

Stephen Peters

In the following viewpoint, Human Rights Campaign National Press Secretary Stephen Peters explains that, while hate crimes reported to the FBI are valuable, they don't fully represent violent acts committed against members of the LGBT+ community. He claims this is due to gender crime data collection only beginning in 2013 and hate crimes going largely unreported. Although Peters maintains the passage of the 2009 Matthew Shepard and James Byrd, Jr. Hate Crimes Prevention Act marked a significant victory for the LGBT community, he says there is still much to be done at the local level.

As you read, consider the following questions:

1. When did the US federal government begin collecting hate crime data on gender-based incidents?
2. What percentage of participating agencies reported zero hate crimes?
3. Why is it important to also have hate crime laws at the state level in addition to national laws?

Yesterday, the Federal Bureau of Investigation (FBI) released its annual Hate Crime Statistics for 2013, including for the first time statistics for hate crimes reported based on gender identity. The Human Rights Campaign (HRC), the nation's largest lesbian, gay, bisexual, and transgender (LGBT) civil rights organization, responded to the report by urging all law enforcement to report hate crimes in their jurisdiction in order to ensure that the state of hate violence in the United States is accurately reported.

"Hate crimes are different from other crimes because they affect not only the victims and their families, but generate fear and insecurity for the entire community they target," said David Stacy, HRC's Government Affairs Director. "While reporting statistics on hate crimes based on sexual orientation—and now on gender identity—are important first steps, so much more work is needed to prevent bias-motivated violence. For example, too many states still do not have an LGBT-inclusive state-level hate crimes law, and we are committed to working with our partners and allies to change that. All people should have the opportunity to live openly, honestly, and safely in their community without fear of harassment or violence."

This year, law enforcement agencies reported 5,928 hate crime incidents involving 6,933 offenses to the FBI. Of those, 20.2 percent of all hate crimes were motivated by sexual orientation, second to crimes motivated by racial bias, and .5 percent of hate crimes were based on gender identity. According to the FBI, more law enforcement agencies in the United States participated in the 2013 data collection effort than ever before. 15,016 law enforcement agencies voluntarily reported their statistics to the FBI compared to 14,511 participating agencies in 2012.

There was a slight decrease in crimes against LGBT individuals in 2013, after increases each year since 2009. 1,233 incidents based on sexual orientation were reported in 2013, down slightly from the past three years, when law enforcement agencies reported 1,299, 1,293, and 1,277 hate crimes in 2012, 2011, and 2010, respectively. (Statistics are published a year after they are reported.)

While this FBI data is incredibly valuable, it does not paint a complete picture of hate crimes against LGBT Americans because of two significant factors. First, under the Matthew Shepard and James Byrd, Jr. Hate Crimes Prevention Act, the FBI only began collecting data on hate crimes committed on the basis of gender identity last year and were reported for the first time in this year's report. HRC remains concerned that the low number of responses for hate crimes based on gender identity and gender non-conformity—31 incidents—suggests that law enforcement are mischaracterizing hate based crimes as ones based on either sexual orientation or gender. Second, current statistics only provide a partial snapshot of hate crimes in America. As in past years, the vast majority of the participating agencies (88%) reported zero hate crimes. This means that law enforcement in those participating agencies affirmatively reported to the FBI that no hate crime incidents occurred in their jurisdiction. In addition, thousands of police agencies across the nation did not submit data to the FBI, including at least one agency with a population of more than 250,000 people, and at least seven agencies in cities with a population between 100,000 and 250,000.

In addition, HRC and partner organizations have worked with the FBI since the passage of the hate crimes bill, assisting in updating the agency's crime reporting form, training materials, and providing details on recent hate crimes when they occur. HRC will continue to work with law enforcement officials and the Department of Justice to press for wider reporting because it is critical to understanding the state of hate violence in America.

On October 28 of this year, HRC and advocates across the country commemorated the fifth anniversary of the signing of the federal HCPA. To commemorate the milestone, HRC released a guide providing an explanation of the federal hate crimes law, an analysis of the effectiveness of the law, and a depiction of the current landscape of hate crimes laws in the 50 states and the District of Columbia. The publication builds on the advocacy guide that HRC originally published in 2009.

The passage of the HCPA was a significant victory in the fight for equality for LGBT people because it was the first major piece of civil rights legislation protecting LGBT individuals. However, as the guide points out, it does not end the need for state lawmakers

The Matthew Shepard and James Byrd, Jr., Hate Crimes Prevention Act of 2009

The Matthew Shepard and James Byrd, Jr., Hate Crimes Prevention Act of 2009, 18 U.S.C. § 249, was enacted as Division E of the National Defense Authorization Act for Fiscal Year 2010. Section 249 of Title 18 provides funding and technical assistance to state, local, and tribal jurisdictions to help them to more effectively **investigate and prosecute hate crimes**.

It also creates a new federal criminal law which criminalizes willfully causing bodily injury (or attempting to do so with fire, firearm, or other dangerous weapon) when: (1) the crime was committed because of the actual or perceived race, color, religion, national origin of any person or (2) the crime was committed because of the actual or perceived religion, national origin, gender, sexual orientation, gender identity, or disability of any person and the crime affected interstate or foreign commerce or occurred within federal special maritime and territorial jurisdiction.

The statute criminalizes only violent acts resulting in bodily injury or attempts to inflict bodily injury, through the use of fire, firearms, explosive and incendiary devices, or other dangerous weapons. The statute does not criminalize threats of violence. Threats to inflict physical injury may be prosecutable under other hate crimes statutes, such as 42 U.S.C. § 3631 or 18 U.S.C. § 245. **Such threats may also be prosecutable under generally applicable federal laws preventing interstate communication of threats.**

"Matthew Shepard And James Byrd, Jr. Hate Crimes Prevention Act Fifth Anniversary,"
The Anti-Defamation League (www.adl.org).

to address hate-motivated crimes that terrorize communities across the country. Every state must consider ways to use state laws to supplement the HCPA.

HRC's guide shows state-level advocates what their state legislatures must do to fully address the problem of hate crimes. The guide also points out several priorities in which HRC is committed to engaging in advocacy and education efforts to bring awareness to hate based violence and to expand legislation aimed at addressing hate crimes.

Several priorities include:

- Amend the HCSA to mandate reporting. In August 2014, FBI Director James Comey explained, "We must continue to impress upon our state and local counterparts in every jurisdiction the need to track and report hate crimes. It is not something we can ignore or sweep under the rug." One effective way of ensuring greater compliance is to mandate hate crimes statistics reporting for local jurisdictions. This would provide a more complete picture of hate based violence in the United States and allow for targeted efforts to address areas with high levels of hate crimes.

- Passage of state laws that protect LGBT individuals from hate crimes. The HCPA only protects LGBT victims from violent crimes where the federal government has jurisdiction over the underlying criminal act, regardless of the bias motivation. Since most crimes in the U.S. are still prosecuted at the state level, LGBT victims remain particularly vulnerable to hate crimes in the states that do not provide protections for individuals based on sexual orientation or gender identity. Passage of state level HCPAs allows states to prosecute hate crimes without a federal nexus and in many instances crimes against property.

- Expand education and training initiatives. The government must complement tough laws and vigorous enforcement—which can deter and address violence motivated by bigotry—with education and training initiatives designed to reduce prejudice. The federal government has an essential role to play in helping law enforcement, communities, and schools implement effective hate crimes prevention programs and activities. Education and exposure are the cornerstones of a long-term solution to prejudice, discrimination and bigotry against all communities. A federal anti-bias education effort would exemplify a proactive commitment to challenging prejudice, stereotyping, and all forms of discrimination that affect the whole community.

Periodical and Internet Sources Bibliography

The following articles have been selected to supplement the diverse views presented in this chapter.

Karen Franklin. "Inside the Minds of People Who Hate Gays," Frontline, http://www.pbs.org/wgbh/pages/frontline/shows/assault/roots/franklin.html.

Jon Grinspan. "The KKK's Failed Comeback," The Huffington Post, November 15, 2015, http://www.huffingtonpost.com/entry/kkk-failed-comeback_us_5654a4dee4b0258edb331a2d.

Alisa Johnson. "Anti-Slavery Amendment Provided Authority to Enact Federal Hate-Crimes Prevention Act," Criminal Law Reporter, April 30, 2014.

Kamal S. Kalsi. "What Does It Take to Call Something a Hate Crime," *Time.com*, September 18, 2015. http://time.com/4035027/what-does-it-take-to-call-something-a-hate-crime.

Reed Karaim. "Vigilante Justice," *American History*, February 2012.

Devin Klios. "15 of the Most Devastating Hate Crimes in American History," *The Richest*, November 20, 2016, http://www.therichest.com/shocking/hate-crimes-15-times-america-lost-its-innocence.

Jack Linshi. "See How the Number of Hate Crimes Has Increased Over Time," Time.com.

Sarah B. Markenson. "What Is a Hate Crime?" *International Law News*, January 2014.

Peter W. Marty. "What Drives Hate?" *Christian Century*, January 4, 2017.

F.S. Pezzella. "The Legacy of Hate Crimes in American History," *in Hate Crime Statutes: A Public Policy and Law Enforcement Dilemma*, Springer, 2017, file:///C:/Users/Owner/Downloads/9783319408408-c2.pdf.

Josh Sanburn. "The KKK Tries to Make a Comeback," *Time.com*, April 15, 2014, http://time.com/63284/kkk-kansas-city-shooting-frazier-glenn-cross.

Amy Sherman. "Loretta Lynch Says Gays and Lesbians Are Most Frequently Targeted for Hate Crimes," *Tampa Bay Times*, June 23, 2016.

GLOBALVIEWPOINTS

CHAPTER 3

Hate Crimes and US Law

We Will Not Tolerate Crimes Fueled by Hate

Edward M. Kennedy

The late Senator Edward M. Kennedy delivered the following address to his fellow senators. He insists hate crimes are a form of internal terrorism and advocates for the passage of the bipartisan Matthew Shepard Act, citing the 1998 incident that claimed Shepard's life as well as David Ritcheson, a Latino hate-crime victim who took his own life after testifying before Congress to promote the hate crime amendment. Ted Kennedy was a democratic senator representing Massachusetts for nearly 50 years.

As you read, consider the following questions:

1. How does Senator Kennedy use the cases of Shepard and Ritcheson to argue for the Hate Crime Amendment?
2. What two deficiencies does the law correct?
3. What kind of prosecution do all hate crimes, including those against gender and sexual orientation, face?

Facing a veto threat from the President of the United States and an uncertain vote in the U.S. Senate, Senator Kennedy fought to pass the Matthew Shepard Local Law Enforcement Hate Crimes Prevention Act. Eventually signed into law in a later Congress, this legislation broadens existing law to prohibit hate

"Hate Crimes Speech", by Edward M. Kennedy, TedKennedy.org, September 25, 2007.

crimes against women, gays, lesbians, and transgender persons; and gives prosecutors enhanced ability to charge and penalize those who commit hate crimes.

Senator Kennedy on the Matthew Shepard Act

I'd like to speak for a moment regarding the Hate Crimes Amendment—at a time when our ideals are under attack by terrorists in other lands, it is more important than ever to demonstrate that we practice what we preach, and that we are doing all we can to root out the bigotry and prejudice in our own country that leads to violence here at home. Now more than ever, we need to act against hate crimes and send a strong message here at home and around the world that we will not tolerate crimes fueled by hate.

Since the September 11th attacks, we've seen a shameful increase in the number of hate crimes committed against Muslims, Sikhs, and Americans of Middle Eastern descent. Congress has done much to respond to the vicious attacks of September 11th. We're doing all that we can to strengthen our defenses against hate that comes from abroad. We've spent billions of dollars in the War on Terrorism to ensure that international terrorist organizations such as al' Qaeda are not able to carry out attacks within the United States. There is no reason why Congress should not act to strengthen our defenses against hate that occurs here at home.

In Iraq and Afghanistan, our soldiers are fighting for freedom and liberty—they are on the front line fighting against evil and hate. We owe it to our troops to uphold those same principles here at home.

Hate crimes are a form of domestic terrorism. They send the poisonous message that some Americans deserve to be victimized solely because of who they are. Like other acts of terrorism, hate crimes have an impact far greater than the impact on the individual victims. They are crimes against entire communities, against the whole nation, and against the fundamental ideals on which America was founded. They are a violation of all our country stands for.

We're united in our effort to root out the cells of hatred around the world. We should not turn a blind eye to acts of hatred and terrorism here at home. We should not shrink now from our role as the beacon of liberty to the rest of the world. The national interest in condemning bias-motivated violence in the United States is strong, and so is our interest in condemning bias-motivated violence occurring worldwide. When the Senate approves this amendment, we will send a message about freedom and equality that will resonate around the world.

Mr. President, hate crimes violate everything our country stands for. They send the poisonous message that some Americans deserve to be victimized solely because of who they are. These are crimes committed against entire communities, against the nation as a whole and the very ideals on which our country was founded.

The time has come to stand up for the victims of these senseless acts of violence—victims like Matthew Shepard, for whom this bill is named, and who died a horrible death in 1998 at the hands of two men who singled him out because of his sexual orientation. Nine years after Matthew's death—nine years—we still haven't gotten it done. How long are we going to wait?

Senator Smith and I urge your support of this bipartisan bill. The House has come through on their side and passed the bill. Now it's time for the Senate to do the same. This year, we can get it done. We came close twice before. In 2000 and 2002, a majority of Senators voted to pass this legislation. In 2004, we had 65 votes for the bill and it was adopted as part of the Defense Authorization Bill. But—that time—it was stripped out in conference.

The President has threatened to veto this legislation, but we can't let that threat stop us from doing the right thing. Let's display the same kind of courage that came from David Ritcheson, a victim of a brutal hate crime that scarred him both physically and emotionally. This spring, David testified before the House Judiciary Committee. He courageously described the horrific attack against him the year before—after what had been an enjoyable evening with other high school students near his home in Spring, Texas.

Later in the evening however, two persons attacked him and one attempted to carve a swastika into his chest. He was viciously beaten and burned with cigarettes, while his attackers screamed terrible epithets at him. He lay unconscious on the ground for 9 hours, and remained in a coma for several weeks. After a very difficult recovery, David became a courageous and determined advocate. Tragically, though, this life-changing experience exacted its toll on David and recently, he took his own life. He had tried so hard to look forward, but he was still haunted by this brutal experience.

My deepest sympathy and condolences go out to David's family and friends coping with this tragic loss. David's death shows us that these crimes have a profound psychological impact. We must do all we can to let victims know they are not to blame for this brutality, that their lives are equally valued. We can't wait any longer to act.

Our amendment is supported by a broad coalition of 210 law enforcement, civic, disability, religious and civil rights groups, including the International Association of Chiefs of Police, the Anti-Defamation League, the Interfaith Alliance, the National Sheriff's Association, the Human Rights Campaign, the National District Attorneys Association and the Leadership Conference on Civil Rights. All these diverse groups have come together to say now is the time for us to take action to protect our fellow citizens from the brutality of hate-motivated violence. They support this legislation, because they know it is a balanced and sensible approach that will bring greater protection to our citizens along with much needed resources to improve local and state law enforcement.

Our bill corrects two major deficiencies in current law. Excessive restrictions require proof that victims were attacked because they were engaged in certain "federally protected activities." And the scope of the law is limited, covering hate crimes based on race, religion, or ethnic background alone.

The federally protected activity requirement is outdated, unwise and unnecessary, particularly when we consider the unjust outcomes of this requirement. Hate crimes now occur in a variety of circumstances, and citizens are often targeted during routine activities that should be protected. All victims should be protected, and it's simply wrong that a hate crime—like the one against David Ritcheson—can't be prosecuted federally because it happened in a private home.

The bill also recognizes that some hate crimes are committed against people because of their sexual orientation, their gender, their gender identity, or their disability. Passing this bill will send a loud and clear message. All hate crimes will face federal prosecution. Action is long overdue. There are too many stories and too many victims.

We must do all we can to end these senseless crimes, and I urge my colleagues to support cloture on this amendment and to support its passage as an amendment to the DOD authorization bill.

Who Monitors Hate Crime Legislation: The Federal Government or the State?

Glen Kercher, Claire Nolasco, and Ling Wu

In the following excerpted viewpoint, the authors insist that both the federal government and individual states have a responsibility for hate crime legislation. They present results of specific cases that challenged both national and state law. Glen Kercher is the former director of the Crime Victim's Institute and a professor at Sam Houston State University in Texas. Claire Nolasco is an assistant professor of criminology at Texas A&M University. Ling Wu is an assistant professor of sociology/criminology and justice studies at Kent State University in Ohio. Both Nolasco and Lu received their doctoral degrees from Sam Houston State University.

As you read, consider the following questions:

1. What are the four forms of hate crime legislation in the United States?
2. In addition to criminal prosecution, can there also be civil action brought against offenders?
3. Which states have comprehensive hate crime laws?

"Hate Crimes", by Glen Kercher, Crime Victims' Institute, August 2008. Reprinted by permission.

Legal Context of Hate Crimes

Hate Crime Legislation

Hate crime legislation at the federal or state level takes on four specific forms: (1) statutes defining hate crimes as substantive offenses, (2) sentence enhancement, (3) statistics collection, and (4) civil remedies.

Substantive Offenses. A defendant who intentionally chooses a victim due to bias or prejudice is charged with a substantive or criminal offense. At the federal level, Congress enacted the Civil Rights Act of 1968 to protect bias victims while they are exercising federally protected activities such as,

1. enrolling in or attending a public school;
2. participating in or enjoying any state administered service or program;
3. applying for or enjoying employment, or using a labor organization or employment agency regardless of whether privately or publicly run;
4. serving or attending any state or federal court;
5. enjoying goods and services of any facility that serves the public; and enjoying the goods, services and facilities of any establishment that provides lodging to transient guests, or of any facility which serves the public and which is principally engaged in selling food or beverages for consumption on the premises, or of any gasoline station, or of any place of exhibition or entertainment or of any other establishment which serves the public.

Sentence Enhancement Offenses. These statutes increase the penalty that may be imposed on the offender if it can be proven beyond reasonable doubt that he or she was motivated by hate or bias. At the federal level, an example is the Hate Crimes Sentencing Enhancement Act enacted as a part of the Violent Crime Control and Law Enforcement Act of 1994. The 1994 Act requires the United States Sentencing Commission to "promulgate guidelines or amend existing guidelines to provide sentencing enhancement of not less than three offense levels for offenses that the finder of fact at trial determines beyond a reasonable doubt are hate crimes."

The statute defines hate crimes as an offense where the defendant intentionally selects a victim or targets property "because of the actual or perceived race, color, religion, national origin, ethnicity, gender, disability, or sexual orientation of any person." Acting under authority of the 1994 Act, the Sentencing Commission amended the Federal Sentencing Guidelines to enhance punishment for bias-motivated crimes. At the state level, the Texas Byrd Act of 2001 can be classified as a sentence enhancement statute.

Civil Action Statutes. A third form of hate crime legislation authorizes civil actions against hate crime offenders. At the federal level, Congress passed the Violence Against Women Act in 1994, allowing the filing of a civil action against an offender who commits sexual assault and other gender-motivated crimes. However, the Supreme Court invalidated this civil remedy in *United States v. Morrison* (529 U.S. 598, 2000), where it ruled that Congress lacked the authority to pass this law under either the Commerce Clause or the Fourteenth Amendment. Since the Supreme Court ruling in 2000, Congress has not enacted any law authorizing federal civil action against a defendant in a gender-motivated assault. Thus, a victim seeking civil remedies against defendants in gender-biased crimes must resort to applicable state laws. Washington, for example, allows "any person deeming himself or herself injured by any [discrimination because of race, creed, color, national origin, sex, or the presence of any sensory, mental, or physical disability]" to file a civil action in any appropriate court to "enjoin further violations, or to recover the actual damages sustained by the person, or both, together with the cost of suit including reasonable attorneys' fees."

Collecting Statistical Information Statutes. These laws require government agencies to collect data about criminal activity motivated by bias. At the federal level, Congress passed the Hate Crime Statistics Act of 1990 (HCSA), to monitor the incidence of hate crimes nationwide. In 1994, the Violent Crime Control and Law Enforcement Act modified the HCSA to include collection of data for crimes based on bias against disability, gender and sexual orientation. At present, participation in this nationwide data collection is voluntary among state law enforcement agencies. An analysis of the hate crime statutes of different states show that there are variations in the groups protected, the remedies available to hate crime victims, the requirement for collection of hate crime statistics and the training mandated for law enforcement. (Only four states (California, Connecticut, Louisiana, and Minnesota) have comprehensive hate crime statutes that include criminal penalties, institution of civil actions as an appropriate legal remedy, mandatory data collection and training for law enforcement. Nineteen states do not provide the remedy of instituting civil actions in their hate crime laws (Alabama, Alaska, Arizona, Delaware, Hawaii, Indiana, Kansas, Kentucky, Maryland, Mississippi, Montana, New Hampshire, New Mexico, North Dakota, New York, South Carolina, Utah, West Virginia, and Wyoming). Twenty-three states have no mandatory data collection of hate crime statistics (Alabama, Alaska, Arkansas, Colorado, Delaware, Georgia, Indiana, Kansas, Mississippi, Missouri, Montana, New Hampshire, New York, North Carolina, North Dakota, Ohio, South Carolina, South Dakota, Tennessee, Utah, Vermont, Wisconsin, and Wyoming). Finally, only 14 states have a hate crime law that requires training for law enforcement officers (Arizona, California, Connecticut, Illinois, Iowa, Kentucky, Louisiana, Massachusetts, Minnesota, New Jersey, New Mexico, Oregon, Rhode Island, and Washington).

Constitutional Challenges at the Federal Courts

In federal courts, constitutional challenges to hate crime statutes have been brought under the First Amendment Freedom of Speech, the Fourteenth Amendment Equal Protection and Due Process Clause, and the Commerce Clause.

First Amendment of the Constitution. This amendment protects freedom of speech, which includes symbolic conduct or non-criminal conduct performed to express a message. The government is prohibited from regulating speech unless it has a compelling reason to do so and the law is necessary to achieve those interests. Critics argue that hate crime statutes punish thoughts in violation of the First Amendment (Corry, Jr., 2000). The Supreme Court addressed these issues when it distinguished between pure thoughts and speech (including symbolic non-criminal conduct) that are protected under the First Amendment and criminal conduct motivated by thought and speech that may be subject to hate crime statutes.

In *R.A.V. v. St. Paul* (505 U.S. 377 [1992]), several teenagers were convicted under a St. Paul ordinance for burning a cross in an African-American family's yard. The ordinance criminalized any display on public or private property of "a symbol, object, appellation, characterization or graffiti, including, but not limited to, a burning cross or Nazi swastika, which one knows or has reasonable grounds to know arouses anger, alarm or resentment in others on the basis of race, color, creed, religion or gender." The defendants challenged the ordinance on First Amendment grounds. The Supreme Court ruled that the ordinance was unconstitutional because it prohibited speech solely based on its content or message. Also, the ordinance criminalized "fighting words" based only on race, color, creed, religion, and gender.

Because the city ordinance prohibited only certain ideas and messages, it was discriminatory. The city tried to argue that the ordinance was necessary to achieve a compelling state interest. The Court, however, held that the ordinance was unnecessary since there were other content-neutral alternatives that could accomplish the same compelling interests. Thus, the city could have enacted an ordinance banning all "fighting words", instead of only limiting the ordinance to "fighting words" that suggested racial, gender or religious intolerance.

While pure thought or speech cannot be regulated or criminalized, biased speech that is manifested through criminal conduct can penalized under hate crime statutes. In *Wisconsin v.*

Mitchell (508 U.S. 476 [1993]), the Supreme Court ruled that the Wisconsin hate crime statute did not violate the First Amendment. Here, a group of African-Americans were discussing a scene from the movie "Mississippi Burning," that involved a white man who beat up a young black boy while the latter prayed. Mitchell provoked the group to attack a white boy who was then walking across the street. The group assaulted the boy, placing him in a coma for four days. Mitchell was convicted for aggravated battery, an offense that carried a penalty of two years imprisonment. However, under the Wisconsin hate statute, Mitchell could serve up to seven years imprisonment because the jury found that Mitchell intentionally chose the victim due to the latter's race. The Supreme Court held that a person's abstract thoughts, however offensive, may not be punished unless those thoughts are manifested in the form of criminal conduct. Hence, the Wisconsin statute did not violate the First Amendment.

Fourteenth Amendment of the Constitution. This amendment prohibits States from passing or enforcing any law that abridges the privileges or immunities of U. S. citizens; deprives any person of life, liberty, or property, without due process of law; or denies any person within the U.S. equal protection of the laws. Section 5 grants Congress the power to enact laws to enforce the Fourteenth Amendment. Critics of hate crime laws argue that Congress does not have the power to enact such laws under Section 5 of the Fourteenth Amendment. The federal courts addressed this issue in the following cases.

In *United States v. Bledsoe* (728 F.2d. 1094 [8th Cir., 1984]), the defendant and his friends regularly harassed victims who they perceived as homosexual at a park in Kansas City, Missouri. In this case, the defendant attacked Steven Harvey, a black male, in the park restroom with a bat, crushing the victim's skull and killing him. Bledsoe then told his friends that he killed a "black faggot." Bledsoe was convicted and sentenced to life imprisonment under 18 U.S.C.A. ß 245(b) for racially motivated interference with Harvey's federal right to enjoy the privileges and facilities of the state park. Bledsoe argued that the statute was unconstitutional since his actions were private, and not State sanctioned and thus, could not be prohibited under the Fourteenth Amendment. The Eighth Circuit ruled that Congress can regulate purely private actions under the Fourteenth Amendment. Thus, 18 U.S.C.A. ß 245(b) was constitutional because Congress had not exceeded the scope of its powers.

Another issue raised against hate crime laws is that it violates the Due Process Clause of the Fourteenth Amendment. In *Apprendi v. New Jersey* (530 U.S. 466 [2000]), the Supreme Court ruled that a New Jersey sentencing enhancement statute was unconstitutional because it deprived a defendant the right to have all relevant facts determined by a jury beyond reasonable doubt. In this case, Apprendi shot several bullets into the home of an African-American family in Vineland, New Jersey, a community that was previously occupied only by Caucasian families. Apprendi admitted his guilt to law enforcement, stating that he did not want African-Americans in his neighborhood, although he later retracted this statement. The New Jersey hate crime statute enhanced the imposable penalty on a criminal defendant by ten to twenty years imprisonment if the trial judge found by a preponderance of the evidence, that the individual "in committing the crime acted with the purpose to intimidate an individual or group of individuals because of race, color, gender, handicap, sexual orientation or ethnicity."

The trial judge found that, under the hate crime law, Apprendi was subject to an enhanced penalty and sentenced him to twelve years in prison. The Supreme Court held that, under the Sixth and Fourteenth Amendments, any evidence that may increase a criminal penalty beyond the prescribed statutory maximum must be presented to a jury and proven beyond a reasonable doubt. The statute allowed the sentencing judge to determine a criminal penalty at a lower standard of preponderance of evidence. Hence, the Court held that it was unconstitutional.

Judicial Interpretation of Bias Motivation by State Courts

A central issue in prosecuting hate crimes is the determination of a defendant's motives.

Under various hate crime laws, the defendant must commit the crime "because of" a prohibited bias or prejudice against the victim. State courts were faced with the dilemma of how to interpret the phrase "because of" particularly when the defendant was motivated by other factors aside from the prejudice or bias against the victim. State courts have interpreted the phrase "because of" to mean that (1) the bias merely contributed to the defendant's criminal conduct (Washington state); (2) the bias was a substantial factor in contributing to the defendant's criminal conduct (California and Texas); or (3) the bias was the sole reason behind the defendant's criminal conduct.

In *In re M.S.* (896 P.2D. 1365 [Cal., 1995]), the California Supreme Court ruled that the phrase "because of" means that "the bias motivation must be a cause in fact of the offense, whether or not other causes also exist." The court stated that in many instances, concurrent and multiple motives contribute to a defendant's criminal conduct. Thus, it would be difficult to interpret California hate crime law as requiring that the defendant's bias towards the victim be the sole factor for the crime. Instead, the court applied the "substantial factor" test to interpret the phrase "because of" in its hate crimes law. The substantial factor test was reiterated and expanded by the court in *People v. Superior Court* (896 P.2d. 1387 [Cal., 1995]). The court ruled that the "bias motivation must have been a cause in fact of the offense, and when multiple concurrent causes exist, the bias motivation must have been a substantial factor in bringing about the offense."

In Texas, the defendant's motive must be a substantial factor in contributing to the crime. The Fourth and Thirteenth Districts of the Texas Court of Appeals clarified that the defendant must have intentionally selected the victim primarily because of the defendant's bias or prejudice.

In *Jaynes v. State of Texas* (216 S.W. 3d. 839 [Tex. Court of App., 13th Dist., 2006]), defendant, a Caucasian male, made racist comments against Jones, an African American while they were at a bar in Victoria, Texas. Jones approached the defendant to question the comments; shortly thereafter, the defendant and Jones engaged in an altercation outside of the bar. During the fight, the defendant pulled a knife on the victim and directed racial comments to Jones before, during, and after the fight. The defendant was charged with aggravated assault with a deadly weapon, enhanced by a hate-crime allegation. A jury found the defendant guilty of the offense and found that the defendant selected Jones because of a bias or prejudice against Jones. The trial court sentenced the appellant to twenty years' imprisonment. The defendant filed a motion for directed verdict and a motion for new trial; both motions were denied. Thus, the defendant appealed. On the issue of how to determine bias or motivation required by the hate crimes statute, the Texas court ruled that the State has to prove that the defendant intentionally select the victim "primarily because of the defendant's bias or prejudice." The term "because of" means that there must be a causal link between the crime and the proven bias or prejudice. By requiring the State to prove a causal link, the statutes prevent prosecution of offenses committed by a person who entertains bias or prejudice but whose bias or prejudice was not a primary motivating factor in the offense charged.

The phrase "because of" was previously interpreted by the Texas Court of Appeals in the case of *Martinez v. State of Texas* (980 S.W. 2d. 662 [Texas Crt of App., 4th Dist., 1998]). The court also clarified two other issues in relation to hate crime laws: whether circumstantial evidence of bias or prejudice may be admitted and whether the victim must be an actual member of the group against which the defendant is biased. In this case, the victim, a two-year old male child, was found lying dead, face down on the top bunk of his bed. An autopsy revealed that the cause of death was blunt abdominal trauma. Martinez, the live-in partner of the victim's mother, later provided a written statement to police investigators stating that he may have accidentally hurt Johnny on the ladder when he put Johnny to bed on the top bunk. Martinez was indicted for capital murder of a child under six years of age. The jury entered a verdict of guilty on the lesser offense of serious bodily injury to a child based on reckless conduct. The trial judge entered a finding pursuant to the Texas Hate Crimes Act that Martinez committed the offense because of bias or prejudice based on sex and race. Hence, the trial judge enhanced the applicable punishment range to that of a second-degree felony, and so instructed the jury. The jury assessed punishment at the maximum penalty of 20 years' imprisonment and imposed a $10,000 fine. The court clarified that the hate crime law does not require evidence of bias or prejudice during the commission of the crime. Circumstantial evidence, consisting of previous racial slurs against the victim, may be admitted to prove the defendant's biased or prejudicial motive. The court held that "the circumstantial evidence must be relevant and reliable to prevent enhancement of punishment for crimes committed by a person who entertains a bias or prejudice, but whose bias was not the primary motivation for the criminal conduct." Although there was no eyewitness who could testify that the defendant used racist remarks during the crime, the court admitted evidence of the defendant's prior prejudicial statements against African-Americans. The court admitted testimony of the victim's mother that Martinez consistently physically abused and disliked the victim because of the color of his skin. The mother testified that the defendant often scared the victim and would poke the victim's dark birthmark over one eye. Also, the mother testified that the defendant referred to the victim as "chingga boy," "nigger baby," or "little black kid." The court also ruled that it was irrelevant whether the victim was actually a member of the group against whom the defendant was thought to be prejudiced. Although the victim was not African-American, it was enough that the defendant was biased against the victim because of his belief that the victim belonged to said race. The court interpreted the statute to mean that the defendant must have acted against the victim's "perceived race or color." It is enough that the defendant believed that the victim was a member of the group against which the defendant was biased.

The Boy Scouts of America Are Legally Allowed to Discriminate

B.A. Robinson

B.A. Robinson, who owns the Ontario Consultants on Religious Tolerance—a website that is committed to presenting major religions and controversies from all perspectives—discusses how the Supreme Court decision to allow the Boy Scouts of America (BSA) to continue to exclude gays by citing the First Amendment may come back to bite them. He claims that subsequent cases and other legislation led to the BSA allowing local troops to make their own decisions about who to welcome and who to exclude.

As you read, consider the following questions:

1. Who was James Dale, the defendant in Boy Scouts of America v. Dale?
2. Was the Supreme Court decision unanimous?
3. Does the Supreme Court ruling apply to leaders and members?

The Supreme Court decision

The U.S. Supreme Court, in a close 5–4 decision in *Boy Scouts of America v. Dale*, overturned an earlier New Jersey Supreme Court ruling that had found that the Boy Scouts were a public accommodation. The case involved the expulsion by a Boy Scout

"Year 2000: A U.S. Supreme Court decision on antigay discrimination by the BSA," by B.A. Robinson, Ontario Consultants on Religious Tolerance, February 1, 2013. Reprinted by permission.

troop in New Jersey of James Dale, a gay male who was an assistant scoutmaster. The U.S. Supreme Court ruled that the BSA is a private organization and thus may set its own moral code. Forcing it to accept gays would violate its constitutional right to freedom of association.

Chief Justice William H. Rehnquist wrote for the majority. He said in part:

> "The values the Boy Scouts seeks to instill are ''based on' those listed in the scout oath and law. The Boy Scouts explains that the scout oath and law provide 'a positive moral code for living; they are a list of 'dos' rather than 'don'ts'. The Boy Scouts asserts that homosexual conduct is inconsistent with the values embodied in the scout oath and law, particularly with the values represented by the terms ''morally straight' and 'clean.'"

> "The Boy Scouts asserts that homosexual conduct is inconsistent with the values it seeks to instill. [Requiring the Scouts to accept homosexual scoutmasters] would significantly burden the organization's right to oppose or disfavor homosexual conduct." He did acknowledge that homosexuality had gained greater social acceptance. However, he wrote that "This is scarcely an argument for denying First Amendment protection to those who refuse to accept these views. The First Amendment protects expression, be it of the popular variety or not." [5]

Justice John Paul Stevens wrote the dissent. He said in part:

> "That such prejudices are still prevalent and that they have caused serious and tangible harm to countless members of the class New Jersey seeks to protect are established matters of fact that neither the Boy Scouts nor the court disputes. That harm can only be aggravated by the creation of a constitutional shield for a policy that is itself the product of a habitual way of thinking about strangers. As Justice Brandeis so wisely advised, 'we must be ever on our guard, lest we erect our prejudices into legal principles.'

> If we would guide by the light of reason, we must let our minds be bold. I respectfully dissent." [5]

Thus the BSA can now legally discriminate on the basis of gender, age, sexual orientation, religious belief or any other basis. At the time of the court decision, they discriminated against what they called the "3 G's:" God, gays and girls. They excluded Agnostics, Atheists, and other non-theists. They prohibited gays and bisexuals from joining the BSA and immediately expelled any who came out of "the closet" as members. For many years they excluded females. However, they do not have to follow local, state or federal anti-discrimination laws.

One interesting implication of the court ruling is that the BSA will now have much more difficulty when they try to gain access to schools or government facilities, or when they try to tap into government resources. In the past, they had held scout jamborees on army bases; this may not be possible in the future.

The court decision only applies to gay scout leaders, "...and does not directly confront the question of whether the Scouts may ban gays from general membership..."[1]

Conservative religious groups applauded the decision; civil rights groups were appalled. Two immediate reactions to the court decision were:

- Jan LaRue, Senior Director of Legal Studies for the Family Research Council, wrote: "It is not the role of government to decide who should share a pup tent with the Scouts, who is fit to be a Scoutmaster, and what message the Scouts should deliver about homosexuality. ... If the Supreme Court had ruled the other way, it could have forced the NAACP to accept a Ku Klux Klan member, the B'Nai Brith to accept Catholics, and the Knights of Columbus to accept Jews as members and leaders. Every private association would have had to look like and believe whatever the government said." [2]

- Ralph G. Neas, spokesperson for People For the American Way Foundation wrote: "The court's decision permits the Boy Scouts to hide their discrimination behind the First Amendment and rejects the right of New Jersey to create a just society for its citizens. The Court has allowed freedom of association to become a tool by which groups unfairly exclude a group of Americans.

"Moral claims have been used to try to justify nearly every form of discrimination against minority groups. The Court has struck down the right of New Jersey to enforce its civil rights laws and upheld the Scouts' blatantly unfair and unlawful practice of excluding gay boys and men on 'moral' grounds."

"Close rulings [by the Supreme Court] this year highlight the precarious future of our constitutional rights and liberties. The results of the [2000] November election will likely change the focus of this Court and either preserve our constitutional and civil rights or turn back the clock for all Americans."[2]

2013: Later developments that might impact the Supreme Court decision

In mid-2012, a secret committee of the BSA reviewed their policy of actively discriminating against lesbians, gays, and bisexuals (LGB). They decided that it was in the best interest of the organization to continue it unchanged. However, by this time, acceptance of equal rights for the LGB community had undergone a rapid increase throughout the U.S.

A surprise development occurred during late 2013-JAN. The BSA announced that it was considering dropping their national discrimination policy against sexual minorities. Instead, they would be adopting a local option by allowing local Scout troops the freedom to either welcome lesbians, gays, and bisexuals, or continue to reject and expel them.

An editorial in the *New York Times* speculated that if this local option to discriminate is adopted, it might have an unexpected impact on the BSA's vulnerability with respect to states' human rights legislation. The editorial said:

> "The new policy would, however, undermine the rationale the Supreme Court voiced in 2000 when it affirmed the right of the

Scouts to discriminate against gay people. The 5-to-4 ruling turned on the court's acceptance of the Scouts' claim that being antigay was a 'core' part of its mission and that its freedom of association right trumped any state nondiscrimination rules. Of course, much has changed since that decision—including the growing acceptance of same-sex marriage and the ability of gay people to serve openly in the military.

Now that the group is on the verge of making discrimination optional, it can no longer claim that discrimination is a 'core' purpose—and therefore state nondiscrimination rules should apply to the Scouts. The halfway policy change would inevitably invite litigation."[4]

A new lawsuit similar to *Boy Scouts of America v. Dale* might result in a reversal of the U.S. Supreme Court's year 2000 decision. The retirement of one conservative/strict constructionist Justice on the court and their replacement by a Justice who views the U.S. Constitution as a living document could easily change the Court's ruling of a future lawsuit from 5 to 4 in favor of discrimination to 5 to 4 against.

Footnotes

1. "Boy scout -- public or private -- discrimination," AANEWS, 2000-JUN-28.
2. "Boy Scouts Not Forced to Pitch a Bigger Tent According to Supreme Court Ruling," The Free Library, 2000-JUN-28, at: http://www.thefreelibrary.com/
3. "Supreme Court Allows Boy Scouts to Hide Discrimination Behind First Amendment Close Ruling Raises Troubling Questions About Future of Civil Rights Laws," Progressive Newswire, 2000-JUN-28, at: http://www.commondreams.org/
4. "Editorial: The Boy Scouts Fall Short," The New York Times, 2013-JAN-29, at: http://www.nytimes.com/
5. "Excerpts From the Supreme Court's Ruling on Gays and the Boy Scouts," New York Times, 2000-JUN-29, at: http://www.nytimes.com/

Hate Crime Laws Can Play a Vital Role in Preventing Crimes

The Leadership Conference Education Fund

The staff of The Leadership Conference on Civil and Human Rights' Education Fund argues that hate crimes affect all Americans. When someone commits a hate crime, they explain, both the victim and the victim's entire community suffer. They further claim that public officials and law enforcement have an opportunity to play critical roles in stopping hate crime through legislation and effective response. The Leadership Conference on Civil and Human Rights and its sister organization, The Leadership Conference Education Fund, work to protect the civil and human rights of everyone in America.

As you read, consider the following questions:

1. When was the Hate Crime Statistics Act (HCSA) passed?
2. What were the leading causes of violence among youth according to the American Psychological Association?
3. Who investigates the majority of hate crime incidents?

For many Americans, the election of President Barack Obama appeared to close the book on a long history of inequality. But the spate of racially-motivated hate crimes and violence against minorities and immigrants that occurred in the final weeks before and after Election Day makes clear that a final victory over prejudice and racial hostility remains elusive.

"Hate Crimes in America: The Nature and Magnitude of the Problem," The Leadership Conference Educational Fund. Reprinted by permission.

Violence committed against individuals because of their race, religion, ethnicity, national origin, gender, gender identity, or sexual orientation remains a serious problem in America. In the nearly twenty years since the 1990 enactment of the Hate Crime Statistics Act (HCSA), the number of hate crimes reported has consistently ranged around 7,500 or more annually, or nearly one every hour of the day. These data almost certainly understate the true numbers of hate crimes committed. Victims may be fearful of authorities and thus may not report these crimes. Or local authorities do not accurately report these violent incidents as hate crimes and thus fail to report them to the federal government.

All Americans have a stake in reducing hate crimes. These crimes are intended to intimidate not only the individual victim, but all members of the victim's community, and even members of other communities historically victimized by hate. By making these victims and communities fearful, angry, and suspicious of other groups—and of the authorities who are charged with protecting them—these incidents fragment and isolate our communities, tearing apart the interwoven fabric of American society.

In one of the most disturbing developments of recent years, some anti-immigration groups, claiming to warn people about the impact of illegal immigration, have inflamed the immigration debate by invoking the dehumanizing, racist stereotypes and bigotry of hate groups. It is no coincidence that as some voices in the anti-immigration debate have demonized immigrants as "invaders" who poison our communities with disease and criminality, haters have taken matters into their own hands.

With society and individuals under increasing stress due to unemployment and hard economic times, a tough law enforcement response to hate crimes, as well as education and programming to reduce violent bigotry, is urgently needed. In 1992, the American Psychological Association reported that "prejudice and discrimination" were leading causes of violence among American youth.[1] Failure to address this unique type of crime could cause an isolated incident to explode into widespread community tension.

Eliminating prejudice requires that Americans develop respect for cultural differences and establish dialogue across racial, ethnic, cultural, and religious boundaries. Education, awareness, and acceptance of group differences are the cornerstones of a long-term solution to prejudice, discrimination, and bigotry. Hate crime laws and effective responses to hate violence by public officials and law enforcement authorities can play an essential role in deterring and preventing these crimes, creating a healthier and stronger society for all Americans.

Hate In America: A 2009 Environmental Scan

Since Congress enacted the Hate Crime Statistics Act in 1990, the FBI has been mandated to collect hate crime data from law enforcement agencies across America. Although the FBI's annual HCSA report clearly undercounts hate crimes, as will be discussed below, it still provides the best snapshot of the magnitude of the hate violence problem in America. As the 2007 HCSA report, the most recent available, makes clear, violence directed at individuals, houses of worship, and community institutions because of prejudice based on race, religion, sexual orientation, or national origin remains unacceptably high and continues to be a serious problem in America.

As documented by the FBI's 2007 HCSA report:

- Approximately 51 percent of the reported hate crimes were race-based, with 18.4 percent on the basis of religion, 16.6 percent on the basis of sexual orientation, and 13.2 percent on the basis of ethnicity.

- Approximately 69 percent of the reported race-based crimes were directed against blacks, 19 percent of the crimes were directed against whites, and 4.9 percent of the crimes were directed against Asians or Pacific Islanders. The number of hate crimes directed against individuals on the basis of their national origin/ethnicity increased to 1,007 in 2007 from 984 in 2006.

- For the fourth year in a row, the number of reported crimes directed against Hispanics increased—from 576 in 2006 to 595 in 2007.

- Though the overall number of hate crimes decreased slightly, the number of hate crimes directed at gay men and lesbians increased almost six percent—from 1,195 in 2006 to 1,265 in 2007.

- Religion-based crimes decreased, from 1,462 in 2006 to 1,400 in 2007, but the number of reported anti-Jewish crimes increased slightly, from 967 in 2006 to 969 in 2007—12.7 percent of all hate crimes reported in 2007—and 69 percent of the reported hate crimes based on religion.

- Reported crimes against Muslims decreased from 156 to 115, 8.2 percent of the religion-based crimes. This is still more than four times the number of hate crimes reported against Muslims in 2000.[2]

The FBI HCSA Data Undercounts the Number of Hate Crimes

In 2007, 13,241 U.S. law enforcement agencies participated in the FBI's HCSA data collection effort—the largest number of police agencies in the seventeen-year history of the Act. Yet, only 2,025 of these participating agencies—15.3 percent—reported even a single hate crime to the FBI.

As in past years, the vast majority of the participating agencies (84.7 percent) reported zero hate crimes. This does not mean that they failed to report; rather, they affirmatively reported to the FBI that no hate crimes occurred in their jurisdiction. In addition, more than 4,000 U.S. police agencies did not participate in this HCSA data collection effort—including at least four agencies in cities with populations of over 250,000 and at least 21 agencies in cities with populations between 100,000 and 250,000.

In contrast to the FBI's HCSA data, the U.S. Department of Justice Bureau of Justice Statistics in 2005 reported sharply higher numbers of hate crimes committed in the U.S.:

> An annual average of 210,000 hate crime victimizations occurred from July 2000 through December 2003. During that period an average of 191,000 hate crime incidents involving one or more victims occurred annually. Victims also indicated that 92,000 of these hate crime victimizations were reported to police. These estimates were derived from victim reports to the National Crime Victimization Survey (NCVS) of the Bureau of Justice Statistics (BJS)[3].

Studies by independent researchers and law enforcement organizations reveal that some of the most likely targets of hate violence are also the least likely to report these crimes to the police. There are many cultural and language barriers to reporting hate crimes to law enforcement officials. Some immigrant hate crime victims fear reprisals or deportation if incidents are reported. Many new Americans come from countries in which residents mistrust and would never call the police—especially if they were in trouble. Gay, lesbian, and transgender victims, facing hostility, discrimination, and, possibly, family pressures may also be reluctant to come forward to report these crimes.

All this evidence strongly suggests a significant underreporting of hate crimes in the United States.

The Legal Landscape: The Scope of Hate Crime Laws in America

The vast majority of hate crimes are investigated and prosecuted by state and local law enforcement officials. In general, a hate crime is a criminal offense intentionally directed at an individual or property in whole or in part because of the victim's actual or perceived race, religion, national origin, gender, gender identity, sexual orientation, or disability. However, each state defines the criminal activity that constitutes a hate crime differently, and the breadth of coverage of these laws varies from state to state.

Hate crimes are generally not separate and distinct criminal offenses. At present, 45 states and the District of Columbia have enacted hate crime penalty enhancement laws, many based on a model statute drafted by the Anti-Defamation League in 1981. Under these laws, a perpetrator can face more severe penalties if the prosecutor can demonstrate, beyond a reasonable doubt, that the victim was intentionally targeted by the perpetrator on the basis of his or her personal characteristics. Almost every state penalty enhancement hate crime law explicitly includes crimes directed against an individual on the basis of race, religion, and national origin/ethnicity. Currently, however, only 30 states and the District of Columbia include sexual orientation-based crimes in these hate crimes statutes; only 26 states and the District of Columbia include coverage of gender-based crimes; only eleven states and the District of Columbia include coverage of gender identity-based crimes; and only 30 states and the District of Columbia include coverage for disability-based crimes.

Footnotes

1. Report of the American Psychological Association Commission on Violence and Youth (pdf), American Psychological Association, 1992.
2. FBI Hate Crime Statistics Act Report for 2007.
3. Caroline Wolf Harlow, U.S. Dept. of Justice, Bureau of Justice Statistics, "Hate Crimes Reported by Victims and Police," (pdf) November 2005.

Law Enforcement and the Legacy of Racial Violence

In 2010, the FBI recorded 3,135 racially motivated criminal incidents in the United States, more than the combined number of hate crimes related to religion (1,322) and sexual orientation (1,277).

A 2009 study published in American Sociological Review, "Contemporary Hate Crimes, Law Enforcement and the Legacy of Racial Violence," investigates the likelihood that a U.S. county's past record of lynchings is associated with lax hate-crime reporting and enforcement today. The researchers, from the State University of New York-Albany and the University of Iowa, focus on counties in Alabama, Arkansas, Florida, Georgia, Kentucky, Louisiana, Mississippi, the Carolinas and Tennessee with records of lynching from 1882 to 1930.

Key study findings include:

- Hate crimes are reported more frequently by law enforcement agencies located in counties with higher overall populations, more police officers on duty, more young residents, and when 40% or less of the general population is black.

- The authors find that hate-crime reporting rates "decrease by about 4% for each percentage increase in the black population," particularly as a county's population exceeds 40%.

- Because "policing agencies in counties with a history of racial antagonism encounter offenses motivated by racial animus with some frequency," they may only report a fraction of hate crimes that occur in their jurisdictions, despite technically being in compliance with federal hate crime reporting rules.

- Overall, a "history of lynching in combination with a relatively large racial minority is associated with lesser compliance with, and enforcement of, hate crime legislation."

"Contemporary hate crimes, law enforcement and the legacy of racial violence," by Margaret Weigel, Journalist's Resource, March 26, 2012. http://journalistsresource.org/studies/government/criminal-justice/racial-hate-crimes-lax-law-enforcement. Licensed under CC BY 3.0.

Communities Benefit from State Hate Crime Laws

The Anti-Defamation League

In the following excerpted viewpoint, the Anti-Defamation League, which has been advocating for the fair and equal treatment of all people for more than 100 years, argues that hate crimes affect all Americans. In their model legislation, which includes gender-based crimes and vandalism, they advocate for penalty enhancements, such as those enacted by the state of Wisconsin. Furthermore, they explain that, without stringent hate crime legislation enforceable in both criminal and civil courts, communities will continue to face intimidation and lack of protection. Key to this goal are federal, state, and local commitments to training, education, and reporting.

As you read, consider the following questions:

1. The Supreme Court upheld which state's hate crime statute that was based on a model put forth by the Anti-Defamation League?
2. In what year did the Anti-Defamation League include hate crimes based on gender bias in its definition of hate crimes?
3. Which federal act allows people to file a federal civil suit dealing with gender-based violence?

Introduction

All Americans have a stake in an effective response to violent bigotry. Hate crimes demand a priority response because of their special emotional and psychological impact on the victim and the victim's community. The damage done by hate crimes cannot be measured solely in terms of physical injury or dollars and cents. Hate crimes may effectively intimidate other members of the victim's community, leaving them feeling isolated, vulnerable and unprotected by the law. By making members of minority communities fearful, angry and suspicious of other groups—and of the power structure that is supposed to protect them—these incidents can damage the fabric of our society and fragment communities.

ADL has long been in the forefront of national and state efforts to deter and counteract hate-motivated criminal activity. Hate crime statutes are necessary because the failure to recognize and effectively address this unique type of crime could cause an isolated incident to explode into widespread community tension.

In June 1993, the United States Supreme Court upheld a Wisconsin hate crime statute that was based on model legislation originally drafted by the Anti-Defamation League (ADL) in 1981.

The following year, ADL published a detailed report on hate crimes laws, Hate Crimes Laws: A Comprehensive Guide, which functions as a reference on hate crimes legislation nationwide. This update is meant to complement the 1994 report and encompasses changes that have occurred since that time, including the League's recent addition of gender to its model hate crimes legislation, and the passage of additional Federal legislation, as well as a description of a number of Federal training and education initiatives to confront hate violence.

ADL Approach to Hate Crime Legislation

ADL Model Legislation

The Anti-Defamation League model hate crimes legislation has been drafted to cover not just anti-Semitic crimes, but all hate crimes. Currently, 43 states and the District of Columbia have enacted laws similar to or based on the ADL model, and almost every state has some form of legislation which can be invoked to redress bias-motivated crimes.

The core of the ADL legal approach is a "penalty-enhancement" concept. In a landmark decision issued in June 1993, the United States Supreme Court unanimously upheld the constitutionality of Wisconsin's penalty-enhancement hate crimes statute, which was based on the ADL model. Expressions of hate protected by the First Amendment's free speech clause are not criminalized. However, criminal activity motivated by hate is subject to a stiffer sentence. A defendant's sentence may be enhanced if he intentionally selects his victim based upon his perception of the victim's race, religion, national origin, sexual orientation or gender.

The ADL model statute also includes an institutional vandalism section which increases the criminal penalties for vandalism aimed at houses of worship, cemeteries, schools and community centers. This provision is useful in dealing with crimes such as the very disturbing series of arsons which have occurred at Black churches across the South in recent years. The legislation also creates a civil action for victims and provides for other additional forms of relief, including recovery of punitive damages and attorney's fees, and parental liability for minor children's actions. Finally the model legislation includes a section on bias crime reporting and training, since accurate, comprehensive data is essential in combating hate crimes.

The Inclusion of Gender

In 1996 the Anti-Defamation League added gender to its model hate crimes legislation. The League chose to add gender after coming to the determination that gender-based hate crimes could not be easily distinguished from other forms of hate motivated violence. Gender-based crimes, like other hate crimes, have a special psychological and emotional impact which extends beyond the original victim. The inclusion of gender is important because it sends the message that gender-based crimes will not be tolerated.

In the past eight years, as state legislators have realized that it is difficult to distinguish race-based and religion-based hate crimes from gender-based hate crimes, the trend has been to include gender in hate crimes legislation. In 1990, only seven of the 31 states which had hate crime statutes included gender. Today, 19 of the 41 statutes cover victims chosen by reason of their gender. Furthermore, the Federal Violence Against Women Act of 1994 (VAWA) allows individuals to file Federal civil law suits in cases of gender-based violence.

After studying the statutes in which gender is included, ADL came to the conclusion that the inclusion of gender has not overwhelmed the reporting system, nor has it distracted the criminal justice system from vigorous action against traditional hate-based crimes. Clearly not all crimes against women are gender-based crimes, and prosecutors have discretion in identifying those crimes which should be prosecuted as hate crimes. Prosecutors also must have concrete admissible evidence of bias to charge an individual with commission of a hate crime. Even in cases where gender bias can be proven, prosecutors may decide that the penalty imposed by the underlying crime is in itself sufficient and penalty enhancement is therefore unnecessary. It is also important to realize that there has not been an overwhelming number of gender-based crimes reported as an extension of domestic violence and rape cases.

Text of ADL Model Legislation

1. Institutional Vandalism

A person commits the crime of institutional vandalism by knowingly vandalizing, defacing or otherwise damaging:

- Any church, synagogue or other building, structure or place used for religious worship or other religious purpose;

- Any cemetery, mortuary or other facility used for the purpose of burial or memorializing the dead;

- Any school, educational facility or community center;

- The grounds adjacent to, and owned or rented by, any institution, facility, building, structure or place described in subsections (i), (ii) or (iii) above; or

- Any personal property contained in any institution, facility, building, structure, or place described in subsections (i), (ii) or (iii) above.

Institutional vandalism is punishable as follows:

- Institutional vandalism is a _____ misdemeanor if the person does any act described in subsection A which causes damage to, or loss of, the property of another.

- Institutional vandalism is a _____ felony if the person does any act described in Subsection A which causes damage to, or loss of, the property of another in an amount in excess of five hundred dollars.

- Institutional vandalism is a _____ felony if the person does any act described in Subsection A which causes damage to, or loss of, the property of another in an amount in excess of one thousand five hundred dollars.

- Institutional vandalism is a _____ felony if the person does any act described in Subsection A which causes damage to, or loss of, the property of another in an amount in excess of five thousand dollars.

In determining the amount of damage to, or loss of, property, damage includes the cost of repair or replacement of the property that was damaged or lost.

2. Bias-Motivated Crimes

- A person commits a Bias-Motivated Crime if, by reason of the actual or perceived race, color, religion, national origin, sexual orientation or gender of another individual or group of individuals, he violates Section _____ of the Penal code (insert code provisions for criminal trespass, criminal mischief, harassment, menacing, intimidation, assault, battery and or other appropriate statutorily proscribed criminal conduct).

- A Bias-Motivated Crime under this code provision is a _____ misdemeanor/ felony (the degree of criminal liability should be at least one degree more serious than that imposed for commission of the underlying offense).

3. Civil Action for Institutional Vandalism and Bias-Motivated Crimes

Irrespective of any criminal prosecution or result thereof, any person incurring injury to his person or damage or loss to his property as a result of conduct in violation of Sections 1 or 2 of this Act shall have a civil action to secure an injunction, damages or other appropriate relief in law or in equity against any and all persons who have violated Sections 1 or 2 of this Act.

- In any such action, whether a violation of Sections 1 or 2 of this Act has occurred shall be determined according to the burden of proof used in other civil actions for similar relief.

- Upon prevailing in such civil action, the plaintiff may recover:

- Both special and general damages, including damages for emotional distress;

- Punitive damages; and/or

- Reasonable attorney fees and costs.

- Notwithstanding any other provision of the law to the contrary, the parent(s) or legal guardian(s) of any un-emancipated minor shall be liable for any judgment rendered against such minor under this Section.

4. Bias Crime Reporting and Training

- The state police or other appropriate state law enforcement agency shall establish and maintain a central repository for the collection and analysis of information regarding Bias-Motivated Crimes as defined in Section 2. Upon establishing such a repository, the state police shall develop a procedure to monitor, record, classify repository, the state police shall develop a procedure to monitor, record, classify and analyze information relating to crimes apparently directed against individuals or groups, or their property, by reason of their actual or perceived race, color, religion, national origin, sexual orientation or gender. The state police shall submit its procedure to the appropriate committee of the state legislature for approval.

- All local law enforcement agencies shall report monthly to the state police concerning such offenses in such form and in such manner as prescribed by rules and regulations adopted by state police. The state police must summarize and analyze the information received and file an annual report with the governor and the appropriate committee of the state legislature.

- Any information, records and statistics collected in accordance with this subsection shall be available for use by any local law enforcement agency, unit of local government, or state agency, to the extent that such information is reasonably necessary or useful to such agency in carrying out the duties imposed upon it by law. Dissemination of such information shall be subject to all confidentiality requirements otherwise imposed by law.

- The state police shall provide training for police officers in identifying, responding to, and reporting all Bias-Motivated Crimes.

Wisconsin's Penalty-Enhancement Statute
Wis. Stat. §939.645 (1991-1992)

§939.645. *Penalty; crimes committed against certain people or property*

1. If a person does all of the following, the penalties for the underlying crime are increased as provided in sub. (2):

(a) Commits a crime under chs. 939 to 948.

(b) Intentionally selects the person against whom the crime under par. (a) is committed or selects the property that is damaged or otherwise affected by the crime under par. (a) in whole or in part because of the actor's belief or perception regarding the race, religion, color, disability, sexual orientation, national origin or ancestry of that person or the owner or occupant of that property, whether or not the actor's belief or perception was correct.

2. (a) If the crime committed under sub. (1) is ordinarily a misdemeanor other than a Class A misdemeanor, the revised maximum fine is $10,000 and the revised maximum period of imprisonment is one year in the county jail.

(b) If the crime committed under sub. (1) is ordinarily a Class A misdemeanor, the penalty increase under this section changes the status of the crime to a felony and the revised maximum fine is $10,000 and the revised maximum period of imprisonment is 2 years.

(c) If the crime committed under sub. (1) is a felony, the maximum fine prescribed by law for the crime may be increased by not more than $5,000 and the maximum

Hate Crimes Against Muslims
Increased After 9/11

Statistics from the FBI show that hate crimes against Muslims have jumped in the years after 2001.

"I was afraid to go outside. If I stayed inside, I couldn't mess up, except maybe with my words, which I policed carefully. I couldn't speed, I couldn't frighten anyone, I couldn't break any law—no matter how tenuous—and therefore couldn't be thrown in Gitmo," says American Muslim writer Shawna Ayoub Ainslie who shared her experience in a *Huffington Post* article.

We looked at data from the FBI on hate crimes against Muslims and found that her fear is not entirely groundless.

Hate crime incidents against Muslims spiked after 9/11

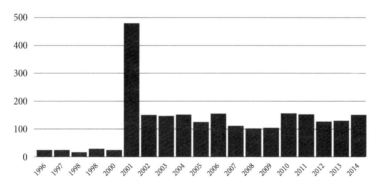

SOURCE: FBI. The latest data is for 2014.

Looking at the figures compiled by the FBI, the number of anti-Muslim hate crime incidents jumped in 2001, from 28 to 481 incidents. The number dropped in the following years, but has never returned to levels reported before the 9/11 attacks.

We also wanted to take a look at the total number of hate crimes to get a sense of the bigger picture.

Hate Crime incidents in the US

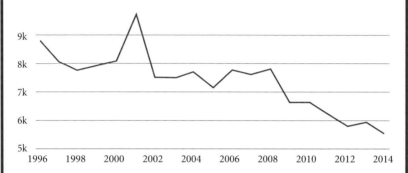

SOURCE: FBI. The latest data is for 2014.

You can see an overall downward trend. But, if you factor out other religions, you'll see hate crimes against Muslims did not follow the general downward trend.

Anti-Muslim hate crimes used to be the second-least reported, but in 2001, they became the second-highest reported among religious-bias incidents, after anti-Jewish hate crimes.

But while Jews are consistently targeted for their faith, the number of incidents has dropped significantly since 2008.

"Data: Hate crimes against Muslims increased after 9/11," by Kuang Keng Kuek Ser, Public Radio International, September 12, 2016

period of imprisonment prescribed by law for the crime may be increased by not more than 5 years.

3. This section provides for the enhancement of the penalties applicable for the underlying crime. The court shall direct that the trier of fact find a special verdict as to all of the issues specified in sub. (1).

4. This section does not apply to any crime if proof of race, religion, color, disability, sexual orientation, national origin or ancestry or proof of any person's perception of belief regarding another's race, religion, color, disability, sexual orientation, national origin or ancestry is required for a conviction for that crime.

Periodical and Internet Sources Bibliography

The following articles have been selected to supplement the diverse views presented in this chapter.

Nancy Badertscher. "Ga. One of Few States without Hate Crime Laws," *The Atlanta Journal-Constitution*, July 1, 2015.

Michael Bronski, Ann Pellegrini, and Michael Amico. "Hate Crime Laws Don't Prevent Violence Against LGBT People," *Nation*, October 2, 2013.

Alexander Cockburn. "Derail the 'Hate Crimes' Bandwagon!" *Nation*, June 15, 2009.

Jessica Hamzelou. "Enshrine Equality in Law and It Will Pay Off," *New Scientist*, June 25, 2016.

Legal Information Institute. "18 U.S. Code § 249—Hate Crimes Act," https://www.law.cornell.edu/uscode/text/18/249.

Brian Levin. "Jeff Sessions Will Be in Charge of Enforcing the Federal Hate Crime Law He Vehemently Opposed," *The Huffington Post*, November 18, 2016, http://www.huffingtonpost.com/brian-levin-jd/trumps-attorney-general-nominee-was_b_13080004.html.

Scott L. Levin. "It's Time for Wyoming to Enact Hate Crime Laws," *Wyoming Tribune-Eagle*, July 8, 2015.

Michael Lieberman. "Hate Crime Laws: Punishment to Fit the Crime," *Dissent*, Summer 2010.

Corrie Mitchell. "FBI Widens List of Groups Subject to Hate Crimes," *Christian Century*, July 10, 2013.

A.C. Thompson and Patrick G. Lee. "Claims of 'Homosexual Agenda' Help Kill Hate Crime Laws in 5 States," ProPublica, February 6, 2017, https://www.propublica.org/article/claims-of-homosexual-agenda-help-kill-hate-crimes-laws-in-five-states.

Matthew Trout. "Federalizing Hate: Constitutional and Practical Limitations to the Matthew Shepard and James Byrd, Jr. Hate Crimes Prevention Act of 2009," *American Criminal Law Review*, Winter 2015.

Eric Tucker. "Q & A.: A Look at How the Federal Law Regards Hate Speech," *St. Louis Post-Dispatch*, January 1, 2016.

GLOBALVIEWPOINTS

CHAPTER 4

Preventing Hate Crimes

Comprehensive Training Is Required to Combat Hate Crimes

International Association of Directors of Law Enforcement Standards and Training

This excerpted viewpoint from the training guide of the IADLEST outlines how honoring diversity is the strength of America's democratic society and the investigation, prosecution, and response to hate crimes must be efficient and effective. The authors argue that comprehensive training is necessary for the prevention of hate crimes and the training involves correct identification of the crime and its motivation. The International Association of Directors of Law Enforcement Standards and Training works to research, develop, and share criminal justice training ideas among training professionals.

As you read, consider the following questions:

1. Can the terms "bias" and "hate" be used interchangeably?
2. How many types of offenders are there and what are they?
3. About how many organized hate groups are there in America?

Bias crimes seriously threaten our democratic society, which is built on the strength of its diversity. These crimes represent a particularly heinous form of physical and/or verbal violence, in which thousands of Americans are victimized each year because of

"Hate Crime Training Core Curriculum for Patrol Officers, Detectives & Command Officers," International Association of Directors of Law Enforcement Standards and Training. Reprinted by permission.

their skin color, ethnicity, religion, gender, or sexual orientation. Growing concern exists around the country, in communities large and small, urban, suburban, and rural, about the prevalence of bias crimes. Crimes such as these, striking at the heart of our country's democratic principles, threaten the very foundation of our society. Swift and effective investigation, prosecution, and response to the victims of these crimes is critical for developing and maintaining respect for and appreciation of the growing diversity of our country's citizens.

Introduction

This curriculum is based on best policies, procedures, practices, and materials currently being used to address bias crimes; existing research on bias crimes and offenders; and the effects of these crimes on individuals and communities. The curriculum was field tested to ensure that it was user-friendly and relevant to law enforcement professionals. The results are reflected in the approach and materials presented in the guide.

Purpose of the Training
NOTE: In this training program, the terms "bias" and "hate" are used interchangeably.

Professionals in law enforcement feel a growing desire to respond more effectively to the victims of bias crimes and to work more effectively.

[...]

Identifying the Crime: Definition of Bias Crimes, Bias Crime Indicators, and Offender Typology

Objectives
By the end of this session, participants will be able to:

- Define what a bias or hate crime is.
- Define the term "bias crime indicator."

- Describe the purpose of bias indicators and how they are employed.

- Identify considerations for the recognition and effective use of bias indicators.

- Given a case example, determine whether bias indicators are present, and if so, which ones they are.

- Understand the types of various hate crime offenders.

- Describe the purpose of identifying offender typology.

[...]

Bias Crime Indicators
Racial, Ethnic, Gender, and Cultural Differences

- Racial, religious, ethnic/national origin, handicap, or sexual orientation group of victim differs from that of offender.

- Victim is a member of a group which is overwhelmingly outnumbered by members of another group in the area where the incident occurred. Victim was engaged in activities promoting his/her group.

- Incident coincided with a holiday or date of particular significance to the

- victim's group.

- Victim, although not a member of the targeted group, is a member of an advocacy group that supports the victim group, or the victim was in the company of a member of the targeted group.

- Historically, animosity exists between the victim's group and the suspect's group.

Comments, Written Statements, Gestures

- Bias-related comments, written statements, or gestures were made by the offender.

Drawings, Markings, Symbols, and Graffiti

- Bias-related drawings, markings, symbols, or graffiti were left at the scene of the incident.

- Bias indicators need not establish that the predominant purpose of an offender's actions was motivated by hatred or bias. It is sufficient for classification of an incident as a bias crime that an offender was acting out of hatred or bias, together with other motives, or that a bias motive was a contributing factor, in whole or in part, in the commission of a criminal act.

Organized Hate Groups

- Objects or items that represent the work of organized hate groups were left (i.e., white hoods, burning crosses), or an organized hate group claimed responsibility for the incident.

- There were indications that a hate group was involved. For example, a hate group claimed responsibility for the crime or was active in the neighborhood.

Previous Existence of Bias Crime/Incidents

- Victim was visiting a location where previous bias crimes had been committed against members of the victim's group.

- Several incidents occurred in the same area, and the victims were members of the same group.

- Victim has received previous harassing mail or phone calls or has been the victim of verbal abuse based on his/her affiliation with a targeted group.

Victim/Witness Perception

- Victims or witnesses perceive that the incident was motivated by bias.

Motive of Suspect

- Suspect was previously involved in a similar incident or is a member of, or associates with members of, an organized hate group.

- The victim was in the company of, or married to, a member of a targeted group.

- The victim was perceived by the offender as violating or breaking from traditional conventions or working in nontraditional employment.

- The offender has a history of previous crimes with a similar modus operandi, and there has been multiple victims of the same [citizenship, race, religion, ethnic/national origin, handicap, sexual orientation, or gender].

Location of Incident

- The victim was in or near an area or place commonly associated with or frequented by a particular [citizenship, race, religion, ethnic/national origin, handicap, sexual orientation, or gender] (ie., a gay bar).

- Incident occurs at or near a house of worship, religious cemetery, the home of a minority family located in a predominately white neighborhood or a gay bar.

Lack of Other Motives

- No clear economic or other motive for the incident exists.

NOTE! The presence of one or more bias indicators suggests that a bias crime may have occurred but does not positively identify a crime or incident as being motivated by bias. A determination of whether a crime is a hate crime can only occur after a thorough investigation.

[…]

Indicator Cautions

Offender's Mistaken Perception: Even if the offender was mistaken in his/her belief that the victim was a member of a racial, religious, ethnic/national origin, or sexual orientation group, the offense is still a hate crime as long as the offender was motivated by bias against that group. For example, a middle-aged, non-gay man walking by a bar frequented by gays was attacked by six teenagers who mistakenly believed the victim had left the bar and was gay. Although the offenders were wrong on both counts, the offense is a bias crime because it was motivated by the offenders' anti-gay bias.

Changes in Findings of Bias: If, after an initial incident report was submitted, a contrary finding regarding bias occurs, the national file must be updated with the new finding. For example, if an initial finding of no bias was later changed to racial bias or a finding of racial bias was later changed to religious bias, the change should be reported to the FBI's UCR Section.

Possible/Desired Responses: Although elements for distinguishing bias crimes from bias incidents vary among States, it is acceptable to identify a case as a possible incident.

Closing Comments on Bias Indicators

Some closing comments about bias indicators that will be useful to participants in investigating potential bias crimes and working with victims follow:

- Often law enforcement professionals may overlook bias crimes when written or verbal bias language is not present, and when other indicators may be less obvious.

- The same holds true with bias crime homicide victims. Frequently, in these cases there are no witnesses to the murder and no one is able to report any language-based bias indicators; this challenges law enforcement to search for other, less obvious indicators.

- Often when a robbery occurs the motive can appear to be economic. However, if robbery is not mentioned or attempted until well into the victim/offender encounter, it is highly possible that bias indicators may be present. The same principle holds true for sexual assault cases. Law enforcement should look for them.

- Remember that the victim does not always understand that he or she may have been victimized by a bias-motivated attack. Often the victims search for other reasons to explain the attack because their group membership represents an aspect of themselves which is not generally possible to change. They will forever be identified as a member of that group and therefore vulnerable to attack. The same theory can apply to witnesses as well, particularly if they are members of the same group as the victim.

[...]

NOTE! Bias indicators have been identified and it has been demonstrated why they are important. Accurate, careful documentation and collection of all the evidence of a bias crime is essential to prosecute successfully.

Offender Typology

Jack Levin and Jack McDevitt of Northeastern University identified three types of offenders in their book on bias crime, *The Rising Tide of Bigotry and Bloodshed*: thrill-seeking offenders, reactive offenders, and mission offenders. (Source: Levin, Jack and McDevitt, Jack. 1993. *The Rising Tide of Bigotry and Bloodshed*. New York: Plenum.) These are not necessarily pure categories, and since offenders can progress from one type to another, the lines between the categories may at times be blurred.

Knowing offender typology helps law enforcement:

- Identify suspects

- Locate offenders

- Gain insight into the perpetrator's perception of the victim's vulnerability

- Gain insight into the offender's motivation
- Determine the probability of escalation
- Anticipate the community response

A. Bias Crime Offender Typology

1. Thrill-Seeking Offenders

Offender Characteristics

- Generally, groups of teenagers
- Not generally associated with an organized hate group

Precipitating Events

- Generally, none

Motivation

- To gain a psychological or social thrill
- To be accepted by peers
- To gain "bragging" rights

Victim

- Almost any member of a vulnerable group
- Members of groups perceived as inferior by offender

Location

- Generally outside of offender "turf"
- Offenders seek out areas frequented by members of targeted group(s)

Additional Characteristics

- Since attacks are random, it is often difficult to identify the offender
- Attacks often involve desecration and vandalism, although they can involve more violent crimes

- Hatred of victim is relatively superficial; offenders may be deterred from repeating the crimes if there is strong societal response condemning the behavior
- Often each group member's participation is limited to a specific aspect of the crime, enabling each offender to avoid acknowledgment of or accountability for the seriousness of the crime

2. Reactive Offenders

Offender Characteristics

- Have a sense of entitlement regarding their rights, privileges, way of life that does not extend to the victim
- Usually have no prior history of criminal behavior or overt bigotry; not generally associated with an organized hate group, although they may call on an organized hate group to assist in mitigating the perceived threat

Precipitating Events

- Offenders perceive a threat to their way of life, community, place of work, or privilege

Motivation

- To protect/defend against the perceived threat constituted by the presence of "outsiders"
- To use fear and intimidation to "send a message" that will repel the "outsiders"

Victim

- Particular individual or group of individuals who are perceived to constitute the threat
- Most often, victims are people of color

Location

- Typically occur in offender's own neighborhood, school, or place of work

Additional Characteristics

- If the threat is perceived to subside, the criminal behavior also subsides

- Offenders feel little if any guilt because they perceive their behavior as a justifiable response to their feeling of violation at the mere presence of the victim

3. Mission Offenders

Offender Characteristics

- Often psychotic, suffering from mental illness that may cause hallucinations, impaired ability to reason, and withdrawal from other people

- Perceives victim groups as evil, subhuman, and/or animal

Precipitating Events

- None

Motivation

- Believes he/she has been instructed by a higher order (God, the Fuhrer, the Imperial Wizard, etc.) to rid the world of this evil

- Believes he/she must get even for the misfortunes he/she has suffered and perceives a conspiracy of some kind being perpetrated by the groups he/she has targeted

- Has a sense of urgency about his/her mission; believes he/she must act before it is too late

Victim

- The category of people he/she perceives as responsible for his/her frustrations

- All members of the despised group are targeted for elimination

Location

- Areas where members of the target group are likely to be found

Additional Characteristics

- This is the rarest kind of bias crime
- Crimes are of a violent nature; the mission often ends in the offender's suicide

B. Organized Hate Groups

1. Group Characteristics

- Range from loosely structured local groups to highly structured international groups
- Many leaders of these groups tend to project a mainstream image rather than a fringe, extremist image
- The significant organized hate groups are technologically sophisticated
- Skinheads, although often not official members of organized hate groups, often support or are loosely affiliated with these groups, taking inspiration and direction from them
- Organized hate groups focus on issues of concern to middle America as a method for cloaking and marketing their hate philosophy (i.e., government interference, cheating, etc.)
- Members of these groups believe in the inevitability of a global war between the races
- Examples include White Aryan Resistance, Ku Klux Klan, neo-Nazis

2. History of Organized Hate Groups

Members of hate groups come from all races. The law enforcement officer needs to be aware of these groups and their common characteristics.

- Organized hate groups are not a new phenomenon.
- Hate groups characteristically grow in numbers and membership during periods of increased immigration, such as the 1920s.

- Periods when disenfranchised groups have attempted to increase their political and economic power, such as Reconstruction and the Civil Rights Movement

- Periods of economic instability when people seek scapegoats to blame for unemployment, such as the 1930s and the late 1980s

Structure of Contemporary Hate Groups

It has been estimated that there are no fewer than 20,000, and possibly no more than 50,000, members of White Supremacist groups in the United States. These groups fall into a number of often overlapping categories, including Ku Klux Klan groups, neo-Nazi groups, Christian Identity groups, and "skinhead" gangs.

Hate Group Ideology

- Explicitly racist, considers people of color to be subhuman.

- Homophobia recently has been added to their agenda.

- Often blame the Federal government, an international Jewish conspiracy, and communism for most of this country's problems.

- Some groups include apocalyptic Christianity in their ideology and believe we are in, or approaching, a period of violence and social turmoil which will precede the Second Coming of Christ.

Strategy

- The major organized hate groups often take a more sophisticated approach to spreading their message, using venues such as cable TV and computer bulletin boards.

- Some are consciously attempting to display a more mainstream image and run for office (often under the banner of a major political party). However, there is always the potential for violence. For example, during the 1980s, a small number of white supremacists formed a paramilitary organization called The Order which was implicated in a

The National Incident-Based Reporting System

The National Incident Based Reporting System (NIBRS) is an incident-based reporting system for crimes known to the police. For each crime incident coming to the attention of law enforcement, a variety of data are collected about the incident. These data include the nature and types of specific offenses in the incident, characteristics of the victim(s) and offender(s), types and value of property stolen and recovered, and characteristics of persons arrested in connection with a crime incident.

Incident-based data provide an extremely large amount of information about crime. The information is also organized in complex ways, reflecting the many different aspects of a crime incident.

"National Incident-Based Reporting System Resource Guide," The Regents of the University of Michigan

number of bombings and murders, including that of Alan Berg, a Jewish radio talk show host. Many of these militant white supremacist groups have relocated to the Pacific Northwest where members have engaged in a number of armed confrontations with Federal authorities.

NIBRS and UCR

The Uniform Crime Reporting (UCR) Program, of which NIBRS is a part, is a city, county, state, and Federal law enforcement program. This program provides a nationwide view of crime based on the submission of crime information by law enforcement agencies throughout the country. The crime data are submitted either through a state UCR Program or directly to the national UCR Program, which is administered by the FBI. Since the 1930s, the data have been used in law enforcement administration, operation, and management, as well as to indicate the levels and nature of crime in the United States.

NIBRS offers law enforcement and the academic community more comprehensive data than ever before available for management, training, planning, and research.

Non-Governmental Organizations Can Target Hate Speech

Organization for Security and Co-Operation in Europe

In the following excerpted viewpoint, the Organization for Security and Co-Operation in Europe (OSCE) outlines how non-governmental organizations (NGOs) can help to prevent hate speech by challenging intolerance. The staff claims that NGOs can hold hate speech practitioners publicly accountable and take legal action. Each participating state, however, has its own laws and must act accordingly. OSCE, an international organization with 57 participating entities across the world, calls particular attention to the internet and sports as centers of hate speech and advocates for increased monitoring and removal of hate from the web.

As you read, consider the following questions:

1. Is hate speech a hate crime?
2. Where may hate speech occur?
3. Who should receive education about hate speech?

Strategies to Combat Hate Speech

Hate crime and hate speech are connected. While a direct relationship can rarely be proven, hate-motivated violence frequently occurs in the context of hateful speech. Organized hate groups express their views through publications, popular music, the Internet and public demonstrations. These seek to normalize and legitimize hate speech and hate crimes.

NGOs can challenge the environment of intolerance created by hate speech. Awareness-raising, monitoring and educational activities play an important part but, in some situations, it may be more effective to denounce purveyors of hate speech or challenge the arguments or claims made by the speakers. In addition, if comments by political leaders and public officials use prejudices or stereotypes, NGOs can take action to hold them accountable before public opinion.

Where hate speech crosses the threshold into crime, NGOs can bring legal action on their own account or to assist others.

Hate Speech and the Law

There is no consensus in the OSCE region on the limits on the freedom of expression with regard to statements motivated by hatred and prejudice. Some participating States criminalize only those forms of expression that represent a real and immediate threat of violence towards a particular individual. In many other countries, laws criminalize oral, written or symbolic communications that advocate for or incite hatred founded on discrimination. How NGOs respond to hate speech will depend on the legal provisions of each state.

The right to freedom of expression has been affirmed in international human rights law, and all OSCE participating States acknowledge this as a fundamental right. Article 19 of the International Covenant on Civil and Political Rights (ICCPR) sets out everyone's right to hold opinions without interference and to freedom of expression. However, Article 20 of the ICCPR states that "any advocacy of national, racial or religious hatred that constitutes incitement to discrimination, hostility or violence shall be prohibited by law". Article 4 of the International Convention on the Elimination of All Forms of Racial Discrimination (CERD) also requires states to prohibit certain forms of speech that advocate racial discrimination.

At a regional level, the EU Framework Decision on Racism and Xenophobia attempts to add further detail to the issue of what forms of speech should face sanctions under criminal law.

The interpretation of these obligations differs widely from state to state: Speech that is subject to criminal sanctions in one country is considered to be protected by the freedom of expression in another.

The OSCE's position on hate speech has rejected the diversity of views among its participating States. OSCE Ministerial Council Decision No. 10/05 emphasized "the need for consistently and unequivocally speaking out against acts and manifestations of hate, particularly in political discourse", while recognizing the importance of balancing respect for freedom of expression with the obligation to combat discrimination.

Monitoring

NGOs can monitor the media for instances of hate speech, while also using the media to respond to particular cases of hate speech and to advance the fight against discrimination and hate crime.

Racism and xenophobia and other forms of intolerance in the media, including the Internet, is subject to national and international legal constraints on discriminatory forms of expression, although national laws differ significantly in this regard.

A number of intergovernmental bodies monitor hate speech in the media, with a view to improved responses through a variety of means. The Council of Europe's European Commission on Racism and Intolerance (ECRI), in its periodic country reports, regularly examines the treatment of minorities in the media while highlighting the role of both self-regulatory media bodies and media complaints procedures.

Politicians

Election campaigns in which political leaders exploit or incite the xenophobic fears and prejudices of the electorate through speeches or slogans often provide the backdrop to violent hate crimes.

In response to such expressions of prejudice, NGOs can press for the application of political sanctions. The expulsion of political parties from regional political groupings is one potential sanction some NGOs have advocated. Similarly, ECRI has encouraged the adoption of legal provisions in Council of Europe Member States that allow for the withdrawal of public financing for political parties that promote racism.

Hate Speech and Intolerance in Football

Racist and other hate speech is prevalent among spectators in many sports, notably in professional football (soccer), where racist chants and harassment of players of minority origin, as well as racist violence, are common. These are frequently dismissed by police and football authorities alike as simply an extension of the confrontational culture of football, not to be taken seriously.

NGOs play an important role in combating racism, homophobia and other intolerance in sport, including through collaboration in campaigns organized by the Football against Racism in Sport (FARE) coalition. Football clubs have increasingly faced fines, the suspension of matches, and other sanctions for the racist behavior of fans, and may also face the loss of government subsidies.

Hate on the Internet: What You Need to Know

Websites and other online environments that propagate racism and other forms of hate are widespread on the Internet. Hate websites are both disturbing and destructive. They are disturbing because they disseminate crude messages of hate, often permeated by violent images and words. The sites are destructive because they are easily accessible and designed to be compelling in order to attract new members, especially young people.

Hate on the Internet is also spread through web forums and listserves, which serve as a vehicle for the daily exchange of racist messages. Hackers sometimes attack the websites of ethnic and religious groups and delete legitimate content, substituting racist and degrading images and statements. Hate-music sites, which contain songs with hateful and prejudiced lyrics, are available on or through links in hate websites.

A significant barrier to police in investigating hate sites that appear to violate hate crime laws is the lack of training on the technical issues involved in identifying who is responsible for hate sites and where those sites originate, and proving who is responsible for the content. NGOs may be able to supplement police investigations by providing technical expertise to train police officers on these issues.

Racist and intolerant speech on the Internet has had a causal relationship to hate crimes. This has included incidents in which hate groups and individuals use the Internet to identify particular people as targets for violence, to encourage such attacks, and to disseminate home addresses and other personal information on the targeted individuals with a view to facilitating these attacks. Explicit instructions for racist attacks on particular individuals are regularly found on the websites of "skinhead" and other extremist groups, despite legal norms in most countries that prohibit such direct incitement to violence.

What can NGOs do?

Monitor the Content of Hate Websites

NGOs that wish to start projects monitoring the Internet can use specialized software to create databases of hate content. This can be used for research, information exchange, comparative work and training. NGOs can also share this information with police agencies, academics, ombudsman institutions, anti-discrimination units or other NGOs.

Advocate for Removal of Hate from the Internet

NGOs can develop contacts with Internet-service providers and become familiar with their policies for dealing with hate sites. Then, by monitoring Internet sites, they can identify content that poses an immediate threat or violates guidelines, and quickly notify Internet-service providers. This does not supplant the role of law enforcement agencies where criminal acts may have occurred but, given the complexity of legal regulation of the Internet, the Internet-service providers may be more effective in removing the problematic content. In some countries, NGOs have been responsible for the closure of websites dedicated to hate speech. They have done so through direct intervention with service providers and government agencies, and bringing legal action.

NGOs have been successful in persuading online authors, owners or Internet service providers to remove hate sites and discriminatory expressions from the Internet, particularly in states with hate-speech laws. NGOs can also offer support for existing or new NGOs that deal with cyber hate.

> In the Netherlands, the Magenta Foundation's Complaints Bureau for Discrimination on the Internet has succeeded in removing thousands of instances of hate speech from the Internet since 1997, by sending requests for their removal to authors or owners of sites containing hate speech. The Netherlands has strong antidiscrimination legislation, and pointing out the illegality of material to authors or owners was enough to have them remove the material in 95 per cent of the cases

Education

Comprehensive guides to education on the problem of cyberhate for parents, teachers and students have been developed by NGOs and are available on the web. NGOs can play an important role in providing training and educational materials against cyber hate:

- **For law enforcement:** NGOs can provide educational materials and training to police and prosecutors in skills and techniques for investigating hate crimes involving the use of the Internet:

- **For parents:** NGOs can provide advice and train parents how to recognize and assess problematic websites, how to transfer this knowledge to their children and how to monitor what sites children log onto. NGOs can distribute "filters" to parents that block access to hate sites on their home computers;

- **For teachers:** NGOs can provide advice on how to talk about cyberhate and how to develop students' critical-thinking skills, which will allow them to ask appropriate questions about the validity of information on websites; and

- **For students:** NGOs can provide young people with information on the dangers of cyberhate, how to recognize and assess discriminatory material, and what can be done against it.

The United States-based youth hate prevention coalition Partners Against Hate published the manual "Hate on the Internet: A Resource Guide for Educators and Families" to equip parents, educators, librarians and other members of the community with tools to help young people recognize and deal with hate on the Internet.

Additional Resources

Brian Willoughby, "10 Ways to Fight Hate on Campus: A Response Guide for College Activists" Southern Poverty Law Center, 2004.

"101 Ways to Combat Prejudice: Close the Book on Hate", Anti-Defamation League, 2001.

Ellen Hofheimer Bettmann and Lorraine Tiven, *Building Community and Combating Hate: Lessons for the Middle School Classroom* (Washington, DC: Partners Against Hate, 2004).

"Combating Racist Crime and Violence: Testimonies and Advocacy Strategies", European Network Against Racism, May 2009.

"Hate on Display: Extremist Symbols, Logos, and Tattoos—Revised and Updated", Anti-Defamation League, 2003.

Lorraine Tiven, *Hate on the Internet: A Response Guide for Educators and Families* (Washington, DC: Partners Against Hate 2003).

"Let's Fight Racism Together! Handbook for Minority Activists in Ukraine = Preodoleem rasizm vmeste! Informatsionnoe posobie", (Kiev: Social Action Centre, 2008).

"Peer Leadership: Helping Youth Become Change Agents in their Schools and Communities", Partners Against Hate, July 2002

Deborah A. Batiste, *Program Activity Guide, Helping Youth Resist Bias and Hate: A Resource Guide for Parents and Educators of Middle School Age Children*, (Washington, DC: Partners Against Hate, 2003).

Michael Wotorson, *Program Activity Guide: Helping Children Resist Bias and Hate* (Washington, DC: Partners Against Hate, 2001).

Jim Carnes (ed.), *Responding to Hate at School: A Guide for Teachers, Counselors and Administrators* (Montgomery, AL: Southern Poverty Law Center, 1999).

Matthew Collins (ed.), Gerry Gable, (ed.), "Signs of Hate", Searchlight Information Services, 2003.

Kenneth S. Stern, "Skinheads: Who They Are & What to Do When They Come to Town", AJC, 1990.

Jim Carrier, Richard Cohen, (ed.) *Ten Ways to Fight Hate: A Community Response Guide*, (Montgomery, AL: Southern Poverty Law Center 2000).

Caryl Stern-LaRosa, Ellen Hofheimer Bettmann, The Anti-Defamation League's Hate Hurts: How Children Learn and Unlearn Prejudice, a Guide for Adults and Children (New York: Anti-Defamation League, 2000)

"Turn It Down Resource Kit", Center for New Community, 2002.

Oppose Hate Speech Online Without Legitimizing It

Gavan Titley

In the following viewpoint, Gavan Titley claims that stopping hate speech online requires identification and analysis of the conversations of young people, complicated by their political and ethical rights to free speech. He specifically cites incidents across Europe involving biased speech against immigrants and Muslims as exercised by thought leaders, including journalists and state leaders. Today's youth, he argues, can reject online racism without legitimizing it. Gavan Titley is a lecturer in media studies at the National University of Ireland in Maynooth.

As you read, consider the following questions:

1. Can young people serve as agents of change in deterring hate speech online?
2. Can imagery constitute hate speech?
3. Based on the incidents noted here, do politicians play a role in both engaging and advocating against hate speech?

Introduction

In an exchange with the philosophers Talal Asad and Mahmood Saba, considering the issues raised by what has become known as the Danish Cartoons Controversy, Judith Butler asks: 'Is the freedom in free speech the same as the freedom to be protected

"Starting Points For Combating Hate Speech Online," by Dr Gavan Titley, Ellie Keen, and Laszlo Foldi, Gavan Titley, October 2014. Reprinted by permission ©Council of Europe.

from violence, or are these two difference valences of freedom? Under what conditions does freedom of speech become freedom to hate? While the first question is of integral importance to these reflections, the second question is one that is perhaps immediately recognizable to youth workers across Europe. The conditions Butler references have many aspects and dimensions, prime among them the resurgent and multivalent *racisms* that have achieved new forms of legitimacy in European political discourse, and the new, interactive and networked communicative conditions that shape their transmission, translation, and impact.

Young people, who increasingly integrate many forms of social media into their intimate, social and political lives, produce, are exposed to, and combat hate speech online. Further, they do so in a context where *what constitutes hate speech, and what is recognized as racism, are key dimensions of online engagement and discursive interaction.* As John Durham Peters has pointed out, freedom of speech has a recursive character, that is, the specific speech issue at stake quickly leads to broader reflections on the larger principles at stake. While the 'limits' of free expression have always been contested, a dominant dimension of the current context is the reworking of racisms through a recursive appeal to freedom of expression. It is this intensely political problem, as much as the range of fora and diversity of targets of 'hate speech' across Europe, that makes engaging with this issue so complex.

Writing about young people is a field frequently beset by polarizing stereotypes; angels or devils, 'change agents' or layabouts, in need of protection and/or discipline. Considerations of racism are often content to locate it at the political extremes, or in the ignorance of pathological individuals. Thinking about the internet remains overly-structured by either/or ideas of romantic transformation or dystopian collapse. When you combine these three fields of inquiry, there is obvious potential for analysis to regard the issues at hand as located at the margins of European democracy. However hate speech online is not marginal, and the edges of this political map are not immediately obvious. The idea of a 'normal region' governed by liberal and rights-based politics is an imagined horizon that obscures a more important view. For that reason, this introduction commences with a recommendation; *'hate speech' and shifting modes of racism must be located in the European political mainstream, and approached as much as a 'trickle down' phenomena as a 'grassroots' expression.*

'Hate speech' is a notoriously difficult concept to define. That difficulty need not deter recognition of how certain forms of racializing political speech have once again become broadly acceptable in mainstream European political discourse. In an interview with the London *Times*, the novelist Martin Amis captured the tone of this impeccably mainstream discourse when he conducted a 'thought experiment', saying:

> "There's a definite urge—don't you have it?—to say, 'The Muslim community will have to suffer until it gets its house in order.' What sort of suffering? Not letting them travel. Deportation— further down the road. Curtailing of freedoms. Strip-searching people who look like they're from the Middle East or from Pakistan... Discriminatory stuff, until it hurts the whole community and they start getting tough with their children."

Amis has not lacked company in conducting such thought experiments. The former Dutch Minister for Integration, Rita

Verdonk, considered introducing a system of 'integration badges' to be worn publicly by *allochtonen*. The now-Chairman of the Finnish parliament's Administration committee, Jussi Halla-Aho, blogged that, given the inevitable disposition of male immigrants to rape, he hoped that it would be 'Red-Green' women that they raped. Thought experiments are, of course, accompanied by more prosaic practices, such as straightforward insult. The then-Interior Minister of France, Nicolas Sarkozy, openly described the multi-racial youth in the impoverished and repressively policed *banlieues* of urban France as *racaille* (scum), during the uprisings of 2005. The most high-profile politician in Europe to be charged with 'hate speech', Geert Wilders, has regularly referred to the Islamic headscarf as a 'head rag', an insult that references the racial slur 'ragheads.' In so doing, it is not clear what differentiates him from the French philosopher Bernard-Henri Lévy, who described the hijab as 'an invitation to rape'; or his fellow *nouveau philosophe*, Andre Glucksmann, who described it as a 'terrorist operation'; or the Lutheran priest Søren Krarup, who as an elected representative of the Danish People's Party compared it to a Nazi swastika.

In the aftermath of the politically-motivated murder of Social Democratic youth members on Utoya, in Norway, on July 22nd, there was a palpable retreat from 'thought experiments' among journalists, commentators and politicians, particularly when Anders Breivik's *Manifesto* was circulated online. In a *Guardian* investigation mapping the networks and links referenced and discussed in what they termed Breivik's 'spider web of hate', the journalist Andrew Brown distinguishes between what he terms the 'paranoid fantasists' of the Islamophobic online networks, and unfair attacks on journalists such as Melanie Phillips, who while cited approvingly in the *Manifesto*, cannot be held responsible for the violence. This is to collapse accusations of direct causality into a wider discussion of the creation of a toxic political climate. More to the point, in drawing this distinction, it is not clear how Brown would account for Phillips' consistent dependence on violent and martial language when stereotyping Muslims in Europe. In her mainstream journalism, Phillips has characterized the émeutes in Paris in 2005 as 'Muslim uprisings against the state'; described a Muslim conference in London in the same year as a gathering of 'racist hate-mongers'; described Palestinian political mobilization for self-determination as 'Holocaust denial as a national project'; and warned that 'thousands of alienated young Muslims, most of them born and bred here but who regard themselves as an army within, are waiting for an opportunity to help destroy the society that sustains them'.

Indeed, the aftermath of the attacks in Norway witnessed a curious phenomenon; the widespread assurance that extreme and exaggerated language and imagery concerning the demographic, cultural and religious threat of Islam—and Muslims—to Europe did not actually mean what it said, or, at least, did not intend the urgency with which it was expressed to be mistaken for real urgency (the kind that could result in action). Here is the Irish journalist, Kevin Myers, who models himself closely on Phillips and who writes for the daily newspaper with the largest circulation in the country, writing in 2006 during the Danish Cartoons controversy: 'As I have said many times, we are at war: a generational, cultural, ethical, political, terrorist and demographic war. Sure we can give ground on the issue of the cartoons of the Prophet by beheading a few Danish cartoonists, thereby giving the Islamicists their Sudetenland.' So when is a war not a war, and what theory of speech is required to understand this process of exaggeration and disavowal? This, and other questions must be answered in a context where, according to a study by the Friedrich Ebert Foundation in 2011:

> Group-focused enmity is widely disseminated in Europe. It is not a phenomenon of the political margins but an issue at the centre of society. Europeans are conspicuously united in their rejection of immigrants and Muslims. About half of all European respondents said that there were too many immigrants in their country and that jobs should be given to non-immigrants in

their country first in a time of crisis. About half condemned Islam as a religion of intolerance.

If the fusion of the 'war on terror' with the anti-Muslim racism that began to noticeably emerge in Europe in the 1990s has provided a particular kind of licence for 'exaggerated' speech, it should not distract from the continued presence of more 'traditional' forms of racist speech in the political mainstream. It is also a challenge to take account of the different forms and targets of racism across the national contexts of the Council of Europe, and to pay attention to how digital communications allows them to feed off and borrow from each other. The Human Rights Commissioner of the Council, Thomas Hammarberg, has issued several warnings in 2011-12 about 'anti-Roma hate speech' by politicians in Italy, Hungary and the Czech Republic.

Also in Italy, in 2009 the Northern League named a December police operation—aimed at checking the residence paperwork of non-EU residents in the town of Coccaglio—as 'White Christmas'. And the examples could continue, but the point is made: openly racist speech is not a marginal phenomenon of concern to young people in online discussions. It is central to, and a central focus of struggle, in mainstream political life in Europe.

It is worth noting this for another reason—when it comes to questions of speech, of defining the content, intent and nature of speech, such operations come up against the unstable and shifting nature of language. In particular, racist discourse—precisely because racism seeks spaces and opportunities for confirmation and legitimation—is shifting and strategic, capable of absorbing and re-coding references, political ideas, statements of value, and in particular, those ideas that are placed in opposition to it.

There is no doubt that the internet and digital communications, in extending capacities and opportunities for communication and participation, have extended the capacities and possibilities for hate speech, racial and bigoted harassment, 'wedge issue' strategies and political recruitment, and the general circulation and insinuation of racist ideas into more and more fora. While 'hate speech' is frequently associated with inflamed emotions and rhetoric, racist strategies online are heavily dependent on strategies that emphasise the provision of alternative information, facticity, and counter public spheres. Thus confronting 'hate speech' and racism online demands mapping and analyzing the various discourses and strategies that young people engage in, are targeted by, experience and confront, and developing reflected practices and messages in turn.

A key dimension of this will be working through the relationship between 'hate speech' and the arguments for control, 'censorship' and legal remedy, and the arguments for 'freedom of speech', but also between what is held to constitute hate speech, and the wider dissemination of racism online. Further, how do strategies of identifying and confronting 'hate speech' sit with the values and practices of youth work? How will a campaign provide a sufficiently unitary and unifying message, while recognizing that ethical and political debates over the nature of speech and its relationship to liberty and democratic life will never be fixed?

Online Hate Sites Pose a Significant Threat to Today's Youth

Lásló Földi

In the following viewpoint, security expert and intelligence analyst Lásló Földi argues that online hate speech poses a real threat to youth around the world. He claims that youth seeking to find a group to identify with can be enticed by hate sites that actively recruit young members, Because each country has its own laws and practices, the author advocates educating the public and teaching people to accept and value diversity. He also outlines elements of successful online, offline, and hybrid campaigns to prevent youth from engaging with online hate speech.

As you read, consider the following questions:

1. What are the specific elements recommended for a successful prevention and intervention campaign?
2. Which two of 10 campaigns noted were cited as successful ones?
3. Which website is cited as an example of building a regional network?

"Starting Points For Combating Hate Speech Online," by Dr. Gavan Titley, Ellie Keen, and Laszlo Foldi; Laszlo Foldi, October 2014. Reprinted by permission ©Council of Europe.

Recommendations for Young People Combating Hate Speech Online

Having been studying the Internet in this respect, it is clear that there are many spaces and an urgent need for further action against cyberhate. There is no doubt that once youth become actively involved in hate sites, they will be exposed to value sets and ideologies that at their very core are offensive, reprehensible, and horrific. Youth looking for a group to identify with will find a community of likeminded thinkers who endorse and encourage such values and who often make practicing them seem like the moral and culturally sound thing to do. The research that has been conducte d and the evidence that has been generated throughout this study have successfully answered the research question: the threat posed to youth by online hate sites is both significant and real. The calibre of hate that exists on these sites is horrifying, and the rhetorical analysis suggests that recruitment efforts targeted at youth are often successful. (Peter Weinberg, 2011)

There is very little creativity invested so far and there is a very obvious need for urgent and strategic action. As concluded from the research studies there are no coherent international legal framework in the world, or in European countries. Hate speech on the Internet is and will be controlled to different degrees by different national authorities. However, the probability of success of national regulations is limited and the result of any regulatory efforts is inevitably influenced by the position of other participants. At present, the international solution, though much desirable, is highly improbable due to differing views on the nature of free speech and freedom from censorship. The option left to every country is to educate the public, to teach tolerance to and acceptance of diverse values. After all, racist speech is a mere symptom of racism. (Yulia A. Timofeeva, 2003)

We have to keep in mind that—as above in Timofeveeva's study—racist speech itself cannot be the target and it cannot only concentrate on the Internet, for hate speech is the result of the malignant attitude of people. So it is the malignant attitude which we can aim to prevent young people from, and support all efforts to change those, who feed this hatred throughout Europe, or even invest into understanding what leads these people to develop that attitude and fight against the reasons rather than the symptoms.

Thus the best solution at the moment is to run different campaigns and projects that, on one hand prevent and prepare young people from and for online hate content and support minority youth groups to run positive affirmative campaigns to change stereotypes and malignant misconcepts.

As for the obstructive campaigns, it has to be said that they can be dangerous for there is no ultimate solution for an absolute ban of the hate content on the Internet. Partly because there are different legal measures in the different countries and internet content can easily travel from one server to another be it even in another country, or continent. On the other hand straightforward obstruction can be counterproductive for it can motivate those who feed hate content to be even more aggressive and insistent in sharing those ideas referring to the right to freedom of speech. It can also be dangerous for young people or youth organisations to get in conflicts with unstable personalities be it virtual or real. So institutionally they can only be put into such a risky context if they are provided the maximum protection and safe anonymity. We should leave this part of the fight to the governments and legal or political organisations.

Ten years into the digital media revolution, our initial ways of educating young people about digital media literacy seem ineffectual at best, and misleading at worst. A popular response is hate filter software programs designed to filter hate sites encountered through search engines. These filters are woefully inadequate at addressing anything but the most overt forms of hate speech online, and even when they work as intended, they disable the critical thinking that is central to what is needed in our approach to digital media literacy. The direction that digital media literacy needs to take is promoting the ability to read text closely and carefully, as well as developing skills necessary to read critically the visual imagery and graphic design. Important in this effort is for young people to become content creators actively engaged in creating their own digital media, which helps demystify the medium in significant ways. And, introducing young people to the regular use of a range of free, online tools for Web analysis is important as well. (Who is registry www.internic.net/whois. html, www.alexa.com web trafficking service, the free software www.touchgraph.com uses a Java applet to display visually the relationship between links leading to and from a site etc.) (Jessie Daniels, 2008)

Based on the overview of the above online campaigns, the following desirable features are recommended to be taken into consideration for the online anti-hate speech campaign designers and organisers.

Type: There is a big lack of real online campaigns against online hate content on the Internet by and for young people. As mentioned already the safest side of online campaigning is awareness raising among the widest public and affirmative campaigns for groups of young people who are at the risk of being targets of discriminative hate. As for obstructive campaigns one has to be aware of the exact legal status of hate speech in the country or countries where the campaign is taking place. A proper institutional and organisational protection must be provided for the young people who are organising the obstructive campaign including legal service, administrative arrangements and safety measures. It is also possible to combine the three types of campaigning, but that clearly implies more preparation, more organisational support and more financial contribution.

Language: The campaign should use the local language(s) for communication; however it would be wise to have all campaigns having an English version so that at the end campaign results can be easily compiled. International campaigns in Europe should be either multilingual or English. The voice and language style should be as close to the actual target generation as possible reaching most of the young people possible.

Target groups and focus: After studying several sites and campaigns for young people it is clear that campaigns should specify the youth groups as much as possible. Just like in professional youth work, there is no such a target group like young people. The specific age group has to be defined. There is a great difference in style, language, message and content with regards to early teenagers (12-16), late teenagers (16-20) or young adults (above 20). Furthermore there are different methods and approaches to highly virtual literate youngsters and moderate Internet users, not to mention the different approach to different subcultures of young people.

Scope: Hate speech is not a local phenomenon, it is a global problem and it affects all human beings. It is an accompaniment, a symptom of a simplified human attitude. Due to the Internet it cannot be solved only locally, or nationally, but at the same time it has to be addressed locally as well as nationally. The scope of the campaign can be local, especially if the type of hate content which a campaign opposed to is local (a local hate group against the local gypsies for example). It can also be national to move legislation in order to criminalize hate speech or challenge a specific discrimination attitude. It can also be European to support the cooperation among EU or CoE member states in order to decrease hate content on the Internet. It can also be global for example to raise awareness of young people and educate them how to encounter hate speech and what to do with it. However it would be very wise to keep the scope of the campaigns as specific as possible for the sake of concrete, tangible results.

Campaign space: There are online, offline and mixed campaigns. In practice it is difficult to define a campaign purely online or offline. Most campaigns are mixed, offline campaigns are using the internet to support the activities, and online campaigns do have offline events. The Internet became part of the reality. We call it virtual space but experts, marketing specialists all say that we handle virtual space just like real life in order to be successful. The campaign organisers must keep it in mind.

Theme: Among the researched campaigns we saw themes like: safety for young surfers, equal opportunities, anti-extremism, anti-fascism, anti-homophobia, equal opportunities, Roma empowerment, changing stereotypes, anti-hate speech...etc. The themes can be very different and it is clear that purely fighting against hate speech as such does not exist; it has to be more specific and broader at the same time. Hate speech is a symptom, not a cause; the campaigns are aiming at fighting the cause rather than the accompaniment. Naturally a fight against online discrimination, or fight against anti-Semitism on the internet will be obviously a fight against hate speech at the same time. However the campaigns should be based on themes around hate speech, for it is the manifestation of hate on the Internet, the words that we read and we hear.

Implementer: The campaigns can be implemented by many actors. In the above cases we saw 2 governmental institutions and 8 non-governmental organisations taking the lead. Only one of them was initiated by young people. Four of them involved young people into the implementation in different ways. It is not because young people are not concerned by this topic. There are two reasons that can be responsible for this phenomenon. Partly fighting hate speech online requires a lot of knowledge and preparation. As we see for example the German hass-im-netz initiative it is a very complex work with a lot professional work in the background. On the other hand the Internet is a free space young people navigate usually to places they like, places they got used to. So those people, who are so to say socially active, would not visit sites where hate content can be found for they are not interested. In terms of issues young people are concerned with supposedly hate content does not have a high priority. It surely does not mean that the risk of facing hate content is not realistic.

Aims: Out of the 10 initiatives two campaigns (All-out, IslamIspeace) had very clear aims and messages, and in light of campaign management these two can be considered good practices of how to campaign online, however they also have lots of space for development. Setting realistic campaign objectives in relation to hate speech campaigns is especially crucial. Clearly defined goals will give you an idea for what you want, and the tools and services that you need to reach those goals will fall into place. When entering into the planning phase it is important to know that the process may not be easy. There will be some trial and error, and results are not overnight. You're going to need to put in work for at least several months before you can start seeing quantifiable results. The most difficult part of jumping into social media is finding programs that fit your objectives and which are effective in generating community around your campaign. Fortunately, there is copious amount of examples and real-world case studies that detail potential social media programs that you can tailor to your specific needs. For example look at the Official 16 Days of Activism Against Gender Violence Campaign on Facebook. Keep in mind that SMART objectives go for campaign planning as well. Objectives should be Specific, Measurable, Achievable, Realistic and Timed well.

Strategy elements: There is clearly a global aim regarding cyberhate, and this is to decrease and possibly spirit off hate content from the Internet, in a way that freedom of expression remains one of its fundamental values. The United Nations Department of Public Information organised a seminar in 2009 with the title "Cyberhate: Danger in Cyberspace." The Secretary-General opened this event and said that *"While the Internet had brought enormous good and transformed the way we live and work, there were also a few dark alleys along the information superhighway. There are those who use information technology to reinforce stereotypes, to spread misinformation and to propagate hate."* He stressed the impact that cyberhate and electronic harassment can have on young people and called on parents, the Internet industry and policymakers, among others, to help stop hate speech and bullying on the Internet and through other forms of modern technology. All campaigns should be in line with this long-term vision. In the European context you have to understand what is going on in the Council of Europe as well as in the European Union. Your campaign strategy should be in line with the global and European strategy.

Role of young people: Young people can play many roles in the campaigns. They can initiate, plan, design, implement and evaluate the campaigns. There is big need for their involvement. According to surveys children start using Internet around the age of 6 in general. In the EU broadbent Internet penetration of youngsters is around 60%, 23% in Malta and 83% in Finland. Children Internet usage is growing rapidly, most notably children between 6-10, and 60% of them were already online in 2008. The tendencies are the same in most CoE countries. So when we talk about the role of young people in these campaigns, we must say they are the only ones who can do something against hate speech on the Internet in the long term. Not only are they the most accessed to Internet, but they are the most competent as well.

Expected results: There are many types of results that can be expected from the campaigns. It can be that a certain number of young people are informed about the necessity of fighting against cyberhate, or a number hate sites are found and deleted, or a number of young people learn how to handle cyberhate in chatrooms and forums even if they are the targets for certain reasons, or it is gathering lobby forces to change legislation, or it challenges stereotypes which can be the bases of malignant attitude etc. It is important that the expected results should also be realistic in relation to the campaign.

Essential features: Looking at the features of the campaigns, a successful campaign involves all possible tools of the Internet. There should be one common campaign portal or some key websites where all the campaigns can be followed. Each campaign should have its character, however in line with a common character. The online campaigns cannot be effective without the use of social media, blogs, video sharing portals and email campaigns.

- Networking gives a very solid and supportive foundation for a campaign, so keep yourself in multiple partnerships, just like all the studied initiatives above.

- The Safer Internet Day campaign could be a stronghold of making the Internet free of hate speech. www.saferinternet. org.

- National and European institutions working in the field of equal opportunities. Anti- discrimination can be involved in the campaigns, and can help in raising funds as well. They also have good resources of information on legal aspects. Look for partners like www.diversite.be, www.jugendschutz. net, or www.inach.net.

- Offline events and offline educational material can support the online campaign very well. Make all materials online or offline specifically user- friendly for the targeted group of young people. In all elements of the campaign, involve as many young people as possible and adequate to make the project a good participation scheme for young people. Like in http://www.jugendschutz.net/materialien/klickts.html.

- In terms of online campaign websites look at www. islamispeace.or.uk and www.allout.org for seeing a good design and structure. The webpage is well designed and easy to understand and navigate. There is no flood of information; the information is well selected and prepared, only the main messages are presented. Connect your website to your Facebook and Twitter profile, where you constantly blog and share.

- Involve real people, with real stories, be honest and straight. For an example look at www.youngjewishproud.org.

- Work in partnership, be local as well as global, try to build regional networks like www.ergonetwork.org.

- Be careful and remain on the ground of facts with hate sites, hate groups. To see an example of researching about hate crime and hate content see http://athenaintezet.hu/en/

index/ or www.hass-im-netz.info or http://www.athenea.hu/ These sites are interesting examples of putting hate speech groups, and malignant attitude into a kind of negative light. With the help of the publicity of the Internet they are criminalized and measured against Human Rights and dignity. Fighting against hate content providers require a systematic and long term work. The content is deleted one day and moved to another server the next.

- For reporting, and complaints see www.inach.net.

- If you gather information and results develop educational material build them in the flow of the campaign.

Laws Against Internet Hate Speech Are Insufficient

Christopher Wolf

Attorney and former Chair of the Anti-Defamation League Internet Task Force Christopher Wolf argues that establishing laws against cyberhate may be the least effective strategy in fighting online hate crimes. Instead, he says, exposing hate speech and how its false language is presented as fact is far more useful in promoting tolerance and diversity. He also proposes engaging in partnerships with the internet industry and together promoting inclusivity and teaching understanding.

As you read, consider the following questions:

1. In which two European countries were laws effective in shutting down Holocaust denial?
2. According to the ADL, what is the "best answer to bad speech?"
3. Which constitutional amendment guarantees free speech?

Introduction

This speech was delivered by Christopher Wolf, Chair of the Anti-Defamation League Internet Task Force and Chair of the International Network Against Cyber Hate at the 3rd International Symposium on Hate on the Internet sponsored by B'nai Brith

"Hate Speech on the Internet and the Law," by Christopher Wolf, The Anti-Defamation League (www.adl.org), September 12, 2006. Reprinted by permission.

Canada Institute for International Affairs and League for Human Rights in Toronto, Canada on September 12, 2006.

Hate Speech on the Internet and the Law

At sessions such as these, hate-filled Web Sites typically are projected on a screen for all to see. Some of the Web Sites deny the Holocaust and espouse virulent anti-Semitism; others portray gays and lesbians as subhuman in the guise of promoting so-called "family values"; and still other Web Sites contain racial epithets and caricatures. Audience members almost always have the same reaction to what they see. When they are finished shaking their heads in disbelief and after they say "disgusting," audience members frequently are heard to exclaim: "There oughta be a law."

Legislatures around the world have heeded the call for new laws aimed at Internet hate, except notably in the United States where the First Amendment prohibits broad regulation of speech. The Internet hate protocol to the Cybercrime Treaty is a prime example of a heralded legal solution to the problem. And even in the United States, while there are not new Internet-specific laws, existing laws against direct threats or incitements to violence or terrorism have been used against online miscreants.

It may surprise you to hear my reaction to the chorus demanding new laws, given that I am an Internet lawyer. In my professional life, I regularly employ an array of laws to go after violations of the law that appear online. I was one of the first lawyers, if not the first, to go after illegal downloading and file sharing of music way back in 1996, long before Napster.

And my reaction also may surprise you given that I am Chair of the International Network Against Cyber Hate (INACH), a coalition of NGOs working together to fight Internet hate.

But my response to the visceral calls for new laws to deal with hate speech is "Not necessarily." I might even put it more strongly: "Laws addressed at Internet hate are perhaps the least effective way to deal with the problem, and create a sense of false security promoting inaction and under use of the other tools available to fight online hate."

To be sure, there are clear cases where legal enforcement is absolutely required. The Web Site of neo-Nazi Bill White posting civil rights lawyer Richard Warman's address and urging others to take violent action against him is plainly illegal even in the land of First Amendment. It is a travesty that the Canadian Radio-television and Telecommunications Commission (CRTC) could not fashion an immediate remedy to protect Mr. Warman and his family. In at least one U.S. jurisdiction, covering California and much of the West, the highest appellate court—the Ninth Circuit—has ruled that specific threats like that addressed to Mr. Warman justifies an injunction shutting down the Web Site containing the threats, as well as millions of dollars in damages. And that is the right result.

And there also are cases where legal action serves to express decent society's outrage against speech that goes well beyond the pale of what is acceptable in normal discourse, especially in light of recent history. In countries like Germany and Austria, the enforcement of laws against Holocaust deniers—given the bitterly sad history of those countries—serves as a message to all citizens (especially impressionable children) that it is literally unspeakable to deny the Holocaust given the horrors of genocide inflicted on those countries. With that said, there are many who believe that prosecutions such as that of David Irving do more to promote his visibility, and to stir up his benighted supporters, than they do to truly quell future hate speech and enlighten the public.

But the reflexive use of the law as the tool of first resort to deal with online hate speech threatens to weaken respect for the law if such attempted law enforcement fails or is used against minor violations. The case brought against Yahoo! to enforce the French law that prohibits the selling or display of neo-Nazi memorabilia in the end trivialized the speech codes directed at Holocaust deniers, and created a series of precedents that could prove unhelpful in future, more serious prosecutions.

Likewise, prosecutions in the U.S. against persons accused of maintaining Web Sites that promoted terrorism failed when it was demonstrated that the content that triggered the prosecutions appeared elsewhere, unchallenged, in more respectable academic sites. Those cases demonstrated perfectly that deciding what speech is in or out of bounds can be extremely difficult, especially when on the Internet the very same content can appear in a variety of locations.

Which brings me to my chief objection to the use of the law as the primary enforcement tool: Given that the U.S. with our First Amendment essentially is a safe-haven for virtually all Web content, shutting down a Web Site in Europe or Canada through legal channels is far from a guarantee that the contents have been censored for all time. The borderless nature of the Internet means that, like chasing cockroaches, squashing one does not solve the problem when there are many more waiting behind the walls—or across the border. Many see prosecution of Internet speech in one country as a futile gesture when the speech can reappear on the Internet almost instantaneously, hosted by an ISP in the United States.

Certainly the prosecutions of Ernst Zundel and Frederick Töben sent messages of deterrence to people that make it their life's work to spread hate around the world that they may well go to jail. And, again, such prosecutions expressed society's outrage at the messages. But all one need do is insert the names of those criminals in a Google search bar, and you will find Web Sites of supporters paying homage to them as martyrs and republishing their messages.

And it must be noted that the cross-border prosecutions give support to repressive regimes like China to request international support and assistance in enforcing their laws, which they justify as important as the laws against Holocaust denial but which in fact are laws squelching the free expression of ideas.

I am not saying that law has no role to play in fighting online hate speech—far from it. I am saying that countries with speech codes should make sure that the proper discretion is employed to use those laws against Internet hate speech, lest the enforcement be seen as ineffectual resulting in a diminished respect for the law. And I am saying that the realities of the Internet are such that shutting down a Web Site through legal means in one country is far from a guarantee that the Web Site is shuttered for all time.

Thus, the law is but one tool in the fight against online hate. At the Anti-Defamation League, where I have chaired the Internet Task Force for more than a decade, we believe that the best antidote to hate speech is counter-speech—exposing hate speech for its deceitful and false content, setting the record straight, and promoting the values of tolerance and diversity. To paraphrase U.S. Supreme Court Justice Brandeis, sunlight is still the best disinfectant—it is always better to expose hate to the light of day than to let it fester in the darkness. ADL has always believed that the best answer to bad speech is more speech. Education is a huge part of what we do, because kids are the most impressionable, susceptible victims of hate speech.

And at the ADL, as well as at INACH, through its member organizations, we seek voluntary cooperation of the Internet community—ISPs and others—to join in the campaign against hate speech. That may mean enforcement of Terms of Service to drop offensive conduct; if more ISPs in the U.S. especially block content, it will at least be more difficult for haters to gain access through respectable hosts. But in the era of Search Engines as the primary portals for Internet users, cooperation from the Googles of the world is an increasingly important goal. Our experience at the ADL with Google the site "Jew Watch" is a good example. The high ranking of Jew Watch in response to a search inquiry was not due to a conscious choice by Google, but was solely a result of an automated system of ranking. Google placed text on its site that apologized for the ranking, and gave users a clear explanation of how search results are obtained, to refute the impression that Jew Watch was a reliable source of information.

I am convinced that if much of the time and energy spent in purported law enforcement against hate speech was used in collaborating and uniting with the online industry to fight the scourge of online hate, we would be making more gains in the fight. That is not to say that the law should be discarded as a tool. But it should be regarded more as a silver bullet reserved for egregious cases where the outcome can make a difference rather than a shotgun scattering pellets but having marginal effect.

Periodical and Internet Sources Bibliography

The following articles have been selected to supplement the diverse views presented in this chapter.

Elaine Ayala. "After Local Hate Crimes, Leaders Call for Education, Sustained Unity," San Antonio Express-News, September 1, 2015.

Leann Snow Flesher and Jennifer Wilkins Davidson. "Can Religious Culture Protect Society's Sacrificial Victims?" *Tikkun*, Winter 2016.

Jessica Huseman. "Inside New York City's Unique Police Task Force Dedicated to Tracking Hate Crimes," *Pacific Standard*, December 28, 2016, https://psmag.com/inside-new-york-citys-unique-police-task-force-dedicated-to-hate-crimes-91e13515f4a5#.upxwisfp5.

Katie Johnson. "Campus Threat Assessment Teams Help to Mitigate Risk," Security Technology Executive, February/March 2016.

Audrey Kabilova. "Racist Internet Forums Linked to U.S. Hate Crimes," Time.com, April 18, 2014, http://time.com/67840/racist-internet-forums-linked-to-u-s-hate-crimes.

Sylvia Mendoza. "Student Safety, Security and Response Time: Is Your Campus in Compliance?" *The Hispanic Outlook in Higher Education*, September 22, 2014.

Joshua Rhett Miller. "Cops Could Start Using Twitter to Prevent Hate Crime," *New York Post*, September 23, 2016, http://nypost.com/2016/09/23/cops-could-start-using-twitter-to-prevent-hate-crimes.

National Crime Prevention Council. "Hate Crime." http://www.ncpc.org/topics/hate-crime.

Elizabeth Levy Paluck and Michael Chwe. "Stop Playing Defense on Hate Crimes," Time.com, November 29, 2016, http://time.com/4583843/stop-hate-influencers.

Southern Poverty Law Center. "Ten Ways to Fight Hate: A Community Response Guide." February 15, 2010. https://www.splcenter.org/20100216/ten-ways-fight-hate-community-response-guide.

Richard Winton. "Law Enforcement; From Tweet to Hate Crime? A New Thee-Year Experiment to Monitor L.A.-Area Social Media Activity Aims to Help Police Predict or Prevent Bias-Based Violence," *Los Angeles Times*, September 4, 2016.

U.S. Department of Justice. "Preventing Youth Hate Crime." Justice.gov, https://www.justice.gov/archive/crs/pubs/prevyouhatecrim.pdf.

For Further Discussion

Chapter 1

1. Both the Los Angeles County Committee on Human Relations and law professor William B. Rubenstein contend that the majority of hate crimes go unreported. What evidence do they present?
2. How do both Rubenstein and psychologists Khan and Ecklund argue that targeted populations cannot be viewed holistically?

Chapter 2

1. What does Peters recommend to encourage states to pass their own hate crime laws?
2. What incidents brought about the Matthew Shepard and James Byrd, Jr. Hate Crimes Prevention Act?

Chapter 3

1. Why is hate crime legislation necessary at both the federal and state levels?
2. According to the Anti-Defamation League, what should the role of local authorities be?

Chapter 4

1. Titley, Földi, and Wolf all maintain that online hate groups target youth populations. Why do hate groups do this?
2. What methods are useful in preventing hate crime according to the International Association of Directors of Law Enforcement Standards and Training?

Organizations to Contact

The editors have compiled the following list of organizations concerned with the issues debated in this book. The descriptions are derived from materials provided by the organizations. All have publications or information available for interested readers. The list was compiled on the date of publication of the present volume; the information provided here may change. Be aware that many organizations take several weeks or longer to respond to inquiries, so allow as much time as possible.

American Civil Liberties Union (ACLU)
125 Broad Street, 18th floor
New York, NY 10004
phone: (212) 549-2500
website: www.aclu.org

The American Civil Liberties Union, established nearly 100 years ago, works to safeguard each American's rights guaranteed under the US Constitution. It has more than two million members and fights against injustices in all 50 states and many US territories. It has a reputation for tackling the toughest challenges in order to defend and maintain people's rights.

Amnesty International
1 Easton Street
London WC1X 0DW
United Kingdom
phone: 44-20-7413-5500
website: www.amnesty.org

Amnesty International, a worldwide movement of more than seven million people, dedicates itself to fighting against injustice and advocating for human rights. It works to ensure powerful groups keep their promises. In 2002, after a nine-year-struggle, it established an International Criminal Court to hold accountable people responsible for war crimes and genocides.

Anti-Defamation League (ADL)

823 United Nations Plaza
New York, NY 10017
phone: (212) 885-7700
website: www.adl.org

The Anti-Defamation League was founded more than 100 years ago to fight anti-Semitism and to advocate for the fair treatment of all individuals. It considers itself the nation's top civil rights and human relations agency. Its mission includes combating hate crimes, bigotry, and racism through collection and dissemination of information. The ADL's mantra is "Imagine a World without Hate."

Anti-Violence Project

116 Nassau Street, 3rd Floor
New York, NY 10038
phone: (212) 714-1184
website: www.avp.org

The Anti-Violence Project offers programs and resources for victims of hate crime and other violent acts while simultaneously advocating for equality of LGBT people and those struggling with and HIV and AIDS. One of the organization's unique strengths is galvanizing communities around violence protection.

Crime Victims' Institute
College of Criminal Justice
Sam Houston State University
P.O. Box 2180
Huntsville, TX 77341-2180
phone: (936) 294-3100
email: crimevictims@shsu.edu
website: www.crimevictimsinstitute.org

The Crime Victims' Institute was founded in 1995 by the Texas legislature. Its mission is to conduct research that examines a crime's impact on its victims and to promote understanding. It also works to assist crime victims and help give them a voice. The institute also provides expertise to policy-makers within Texas. Its current research agenda focuses on sexual assault and human trafficking.

Human Rights First
805 15th Street, NW
Suite 900
Washington, DC 20005-2207
phone: (202) 370-3323
website: www.humanrightsfirst.org

Human Rights First is an international organization that helps to protect those at risk, including victims of discrimination and hate crime. It offers a Fighting Discrimination Program to specifically address government actions that are racist, anti-Semitic, anti-Muslim, xenophobic, and homophobic, and other biased acts of violence.

Matthew Shepard Foundation
800 18th Street, Suite 101
Denver, CO 80202
phone: (303) 830-7400
website: www.matthewshepard.org

The Matthew Shepard Foundation was founded in 1998 in memory of Matthew Shepard, who was murdered in an anti-gay hate crime in Wyoming. The organization, founded by Matthew's parents, Dennis and Judy, works to eliminate hate, help foster environments where young people can feel safe, and advocate for equality for all LGBT+ people in America.

National Gay and Lesbian Task Force
1325 Massachusetts Ave., NW
Suite 600
Washington, DC 20005
phone: (202) 393-5177
website: www.thetaskforce.org

With offices in Washington, DC, New York, Cambridge, Miami, and Minneapolis, the National Gay and Lesbian Task Force advocates for gay rights. It also monitors hate crimes and issues statistics and reports on hate crime status by state and on hate crime legislation.

National Organization for Victim Assistance (NOVA)
510 King Street, Suite 424
Alexandria, VA 22314
phone: (703) 535-6682
website: www.trynova.org

The National Organization for Victim Assistance was founded in 1975 and is the leading organization in advocating for and helping victims of crisis and crime, including hate crime. This nonprofit organization offers resources and training.

Organization for Security & Co-operation in Europe (OSCE)
Wallnerstrasse 6
1010 Vienna
Austria
phone: 43-1-514-360
website: www.osce.org

The OSCE works to ensure politico-military, economic, environment, and human security across its 57 participating states in Europe, North America, and Central Asia. Among its many initiatives, it fights to counter terrorism and advocates for human rights and keeping national minorities safe. It offers many documents and publications that target hate crime.

Southern Poverty Law Center
400 Washington Avenue
Montgomery, AL 36104
phone: (334) 956-8200 or (888) 414-7752
website: www.splcenter.org

The Southern Poverty Law Center develops tolerance education programs for its fight against discrimination. It has a particular focus on hate crimes and offers documentation of hate crime incidents.

Stop Hate UK
P. O. Box 851
Leeds LS1 9QS
United Kingdom
phone: 0113-293-5100
email: info@stophateuk.org
website: www.stophateuk.org

Stop Hate UK was founded in 1995 in response to the murder of Stephen Lawrence, a victim of racial hate. It offers reporting and support for victims, witnesses, and others. The organization sponsors a National Hate Crime Week and provides specific support to LGBT victims of hate crimes and those with learning disabilities.

US Federal Bureau of Investigation (FBI)
935 Pennsylvania Avenue, NW
Washington, DC 20535-0001
phone: (202) 324-3000
website: www.fbi.gov

The FBI serves a multifaceted role with respect to hate crime. It investigates crimes, supports local law enforcement, works with prosecutors to hold those responsible for the crimes accountable for their actions, partners with many organizations to protect communities, and offers training.

US National Criminal Justice Reference Service (NCJRS)
P.O. Box 6000
Rockville, MD 20849-6000
phone: (800) 851-3420
email: responsecenter@ncjrs.gov
website: www.ncjrs.gov

The NCJRS, founded in 1972, offers resources to support research, policy, and program development. Although a federal service based in the United States, it serves people worldwide. It is sponsored by the US Justice Department.

Bibliography of Books

Ely Aaronson. *From Slave Abuse to Hate Crime: The Criminalization of Racial Violence in American History.* Cambridge, UK: Cambridge University Press, 2014.

Donald Altschiller. *Hate Crimes: A Reference Handbook.* Santa Barbara, CA: ABC-CLIO, 2015.

Neil Chakraborti and Jon Garland. *Hate Crime: Impact, Causes & Responses.* Los Angeles, CA: SAGE, 2016.

Neil Chakraborti and Jon Garland. *Responding to Hate Crime: The Case for Connecting Policy and Research.* Bristol, UK: Policy Press, 2014.

Danielle Keats Citron. *Hate Crimes in Cyberspace.* Cambridge, MA: Harvard University Press, 2016.

Marian Duggan and Vicky Heap. *Administrating Victimization: The Politics of Anti-Social Behavior and Hate Crime.* Basingstoke, UK: Palgrave Macmillan, 2014.

Edward Dunbar, Amalio Blanco Abarca, Desirée A. Crèvecoeur-MacPhail, and Christian Munthe. *The Psychology of Hate Crimes as Domestic Terrorism: U.S. and Global Issues.* Santa Barbara, CA: Praeger, 2017.

Phyllis B. Gerstenfeld. *Hate Crimes: Causes, Controls, and Controversies, Fourth Edition.* Thousand Oaks, CA: Sage Publications, 2018.

Nathan Hall. *The Routledge International Handbook on Hate Crime.* New York, NY: Routledge, 2015.

Teo Keipi, Matti Näsi, Atte Oksanen, and Pekka Räsänen. *Online Hate and Harmful Content: Cross-National Perspectives.* New York, NY: Routledge, 2017.

Clara S. Lewis. *Tough on Hate? The Cultural Politics of Hate Crimes.* New Brunswick, NJ: Rutgers University Press, 2014.

Allyson Lunny. *Debating Hate Crime: Language.* Vancouver, Canada: University of British Columbia Press, 2015.

Gail Mason, JaneMaree Maher, Jude McCulloch, Sharon Pickering, Rebecca Wickes, and Carolyn McKay. *Policing Hate Crime: Understanding Communities and Prejudice.* New York, NY: Routledge, 2017.

Victoria Munro. *Hate Crime in the Media: A History.* Santa Barbara, CA: Praeger, 2014.

National Center for Victims of Crime, United States Office of Justice Programs, and Office for Victims of Crime. *Hate and Bias Crime.* Washington, DC: Office for Victims of Crime, 2016.

Michael Newton. *Hate Crime in America, 1968-2013: A Chronicling of Offenses, Legislation, and Related Events.* Jefferson, NC: McFarland, 2014.

Michael Newton. *Ku Klux Klan: History, Organization, Language, Influence and Activities of America's Most Notorious Secret Society.* Jefferson, NC: McFarland, 2014.

Elaine Frantz Parsons. *Ku-Klux: The Birth of the Klan during Reconstruction.* Chapel Hill, NC: University of North Carolina Press, 2016.

Frank S. Pezzella. *Hate Crime Statutes: A Public Policy and Law Enforcement Dilemma.* New York, NY: Springer, 2016.

Mark Paul Richard. *The Ku Klux Klan Confronts New England in the 1920s.* Amherst, MA: University of Massachusetts Press, 2015.

Alan Roulstone and Hannah Mason-Bish. *Disability, Hate Crime and Violence.* London, UK: Routledge, 2014.

Nathan Sandholz, Lynn Langton, Mike Planty, and United States Bureau of Justice Statistics. *Hate Crime Victimization, 2003-2011.* Washington, DC: US Department of Justice, Office of Justice Programs, Bureau of Justice Statistics, 2013.

Jennifer Schweppe and Mark Austin Walters, Eds. *The Globalization of Hate: Internationalizing Hate Crime?* Oxford, UK: Oxford University Press, 2016.

Robina Shah and Paul Giannasi. *Tackling Disability Discrimination and Disability Hate Crime: A Multidisciplinary Guide.* Philadelphia, PA: Jessica Kingsley Publishers, 2015.

Judy Shepard. *The Meaning of Matthew: My Son's Murder in Laramie, and a World Transformed.* New York, NY: Plume, 2014.

Mary E. Swigonski, Robin S. Mama, and Kelly Ward, Eds. *From Hate to Human Rights: A Tribute to Matthew Shepard.* New York, NY: Routledge, 2013.

Carolyn Turpin-Petrosino. *Understanding Hate Crimes: Acts, Motives, Offenses, Victims and Justice.* London, UK: Routledge, 2015.

Mark Austin Walters. *Hate Crime and Restorative Justice: Exploring Causes, Repairing Harms.* Oxford, UK: Oxford University Press, 2014.

Index